Wycliffe
Preparatory School
Library

08121

The Preparatory Schools' Cricket Almanac

2006

The Preparatory Schools' Cricket Almanac

2006

Edited by
Andrew Fraser and Grenville Simons

Foreword by
Chris Cowdrey

Wisteria Books

Birtsmorton

First published in 2006

by
Wisteria Books
Wisteria Cottage
Birt Street
Birtsmorton
Malvern
Worcs. WR13 6AW
www.wisteriabooks.co.uk

Copyright © Andrew Fraser and Grenville Simons 2006

British Library Cataloguing in Publication Data

ISBN 0 9527760 4 9

All Rights Reserved. No part of this publication may be
reproduced, stored in a retrieval system, or transmitted, in any
form or by any means, electronic, mechanical, photocopying,
recording or otherwise, without prior permission of the author.

Design and Typesetting by George Simons

Set in Times and Din-Medium 10/9/8/7

Printed by Aldine Print Ltd., Malvern

Bound by JWB Finishers Ltd., Wolverhampton

CONTENTS

continued

(In all team lists * denotes colours)

Illustrations

FOREWORD

by Chris Cowdrey

What fun it was to delve into the first *Preparatory Schools'*
Cricket Almanac in 2005. It brought back vivid memories of my
own experiences as a prep school boy at Wellesley House. The
sound of the mower preparing for the afternoon match and the
whiff of cut grass drifting through the open window during
Latin. The darkening of the classroom as a cloud temporarily
shades the sun – surely not rain on a match day. The tension in
the stomach as the butterflies start to kick in. The smell of lunch
- hooray - not long to go.

The Almanac reminded me how fortunate I was to take part
in the greatest team sport at such a young age, yet it saddens me
that so few children have this opportunity. How wonderful for a
youngster at Millfield to play twenty-five matches in a summer
term, for boys at Caldicott to aspire to their former pupil
Andrew Strauss, or those as far afield as Craigclowan, to learn
of the treasured values of cricket.

It is important that credit is given to the team player in the
Almanac, even when the prep school game inevitably becomes
solely a limited-overs contest. The boy with the best average
will not always be the most valuable member of the team.
Whoever submits the reports might also consider the
exceptional fielder – it has always been a mystery to me that we
have not yet devised a method to give statistical credit to a
fielder.

I believe that schools should play a mixture of conventional
and limited over cricket. An imbalance of batting time can even
up a contest, but the emphasis is all too often on a draw from
the outset, achieving more for the ego or CV of a master-in-
charge, than the cricket education of a team. The limited overs
match offers greater opportunity to more players, which should
be a priority, ahead of the modern day culture of winning at any
cost. If Australia can buy into 'the Spirit of Cricket' so can our
preparatory schools.

For several years the Cowdrey Cricket Class have coached 4 to 13-year-olds in the school holidays. The main emphasis is in the summer, when pupils break up full of enthusiasm for cricket, yet with little available. We are free from football for three weeks a year (July/August) to concentrate on our summer game, yet coaches and match managers go abroad bemoaning that they cannot raise a team in the summer holidays. Such apathy must be addressed. The good example set by the preparatory schools must again be reflected in the clubs, parks, sports halls, back streets and ultimately all schools.

Who knows, we may still hold the Ashes when the next boy from within these pages represents the full England team.

Chris Cowdrey
November 2005

EDITORIAL

What an extraordinary summer! The football season was put on hold, strangers at airports shared the latest scores with others, supporters who had paid good money applauded umpires leaving the field for bad light, cricket bat sales rose by seventy per cent and city trading floors roared their approval of every run and wicket to the bemusement of continental staff. For those of us who teach and love cricket it was manna from heaven.

The series showed a remarkable degree of sportsmanship, on both sides, and it was clear that this came from the players themselves. They are not the overpaid prima donnas of elsewhere in the sporting world, nor are they the gentry of yesteryear. They played to the edge of the laws but rarely beyond, they applauded other players successes, even those of the opposition, they had poor sessions but bounced back in the next, they supported each other through good and bad. One by one the England team produced performances when they were really required. Ultimately they were a team and that spirit won through. Theirs was an example of how cricket should be played and a wonderful reinforcement of the values which should underpin the coaching of cricket at school level and upon which we touched in last year's editorial.

For the PSCA it has also been an amazing year. The response to the first edition was heart-warming, from retired teachers to players' mothers, and made all the effort worthwhile. This year we have more schools in the Almanac, including our first overseas entry, and we are publishing the first edition of *The Schools' Cricket Almanac* for 1st XIs at U18 level. We look forward to seeing cricketers featured in the PSCA making their mark at that level in years to come.

Our thanks must go to the many who help in making the PSCA a success. The teachers and coaches in our schools are key to the long-term future of the publication. Please continue to spread the word amongst the many schools whose names feature only as opposition and let us know if you are hosting or attending a tournament or event which could feature in the 2007 edition. We welcome suggestions and criticisms and would gratefully receive any articles or photographs about preparatory school cricket.

Sincere thanks also to Chris Cowdrey for his foreword, to Neil Rattee and John Maurice for their recollections of 'Crusoe', to John Barclay, John Bampfield, David Bromwich and Andrew Baker, and to all those who have assisted or supported us with the 2006 edition.

Andrew Fraser and Grenville Simons January 2006

The Editors, PSCA, 2 Malvern Cottages, Stowe Lane, Colwall, Nr. Malvern, Worcs. WR13 6EH Tel 01684 541167 or Tel/Fax 01684 833578
Email psca@wisteriabooks.co.uk www.wisteriabooks.co.uk

ABBERLEY HALL

Worcester, WR6 6DD

Tel: 01299 896275 Fax: 01299 896875

Email: postmaster@abberleyhall.co.uk

Headmaster: J.G.W. Walker Master i/c Cricket: Alastair Wilkes

2005 SEASON

Played: 11   Won: 3   Lost: 4   Drawn: 4

Captain: W. Gough

Team selected from: W. Gough, J. Angell-James*, W. Griffee, R. Green, A. Mason, F. Parry, J. Townley, R. Powers, C. Lowe, R. Mucklow, T. Wills, J. Lovett, D. Hackett, Z. Yarranton.

SUMMARY

This was a rollercoaster of a season. There were several highs - notably a rare victory against Packwood Haugh and an excellent run-chase at home to Wycliffe. Off-spinner Jack Angell-James was a constant threat but he lacked any real support.

There were also, however, a number of lows. We collapsed at home to RGS Worcester, were hit to all parts at Bromsgrove and having fielded splendidly against Clifton Durban, we then capitulated to an embarrassing defeat. The top seven batsmen all scored over 30 but no one did it on a regular basis.

It is encouraging that half the team will be back next year and all have real potential.

AVERAGES

BATSMAN	INNINGS	NOT OUT	RUNS	H. SCORE	AVERAGE
A. Mason	11	1	170	59	17.0
F. Parry	10	1	144	50*	16.0

BOWLER	OVERS	MAIDENS	RUNS	WICKETS	AVERAGE
J. Angell-James	96	12	256	32	8.0
R. Powers	49	10	180	9	20.0

WICKET-KEEPER	PLAYED	CAUGHT	STUMPED
C. Lowe	8	5	1

NOTABLE BATTING PERFORMANCES

PLAYER	OPPOSITION	SCORE
F. Parry	Wycliffe	50*
R. Green	Arnold Lodge	51
A. Mason	Birchfield	59
J. Townley	Packwood Haugh	40*

NOTABLE BOWLING PERFORMANCES

PLAYER	OPPOSITION	FIGURES
J. Angell-James	Cheltenham College	6-37
J. Angell-James	Arnold Lodge	4-2
R. Powers	Wycliffe	3-9

Did you know? . . . Following on from England's victorious summer, all the 'Did you knows' in this year's Almanac are related to Ashes Test cricket.

ALDRO

Lombard Street, Shackleford, Godalming, Surrey GU8 6AS

Tel: 01483 810266 Fax: 01483 409001

Email: hmsec@aldro.org

Headmaster: D.W.N. Aston   Master i/c Cricket: C. Rose

2005 SEASON

Played: 13   Won: 7   Lost: 4   Drawn: 2

Captain: C. Pickard

Team selected from: C. Pickard*, J. Wynne-Griffith*,
G. Quaile*, O. Davies, C. Fletcher, D. MacFarlane, C. Court,
C. Russell-Jones, J. Buck, A. Corridan, N. Pattinson, A. Creed.

Scorer: W. Mitchell

SUMMARY

A hugely enjoyable season saw the first five matches yield just two draws. Thereafter the team won seven of its next eight games. Some high scores were posted: 155-0 at St. Andrew's Woking, 144-7 versus Westbourne House, 176-4 playing against Lanesborough and 178-5 in the face of a strong Edgeborough bowling attack. Highlights included victories over Hoe Bridge and Hall Grove, and a Twenty20 triumph over a previously undefeated Millfield side.

Charlie Pickard led from the front, scoring over 400 runs, including an unbeaten century against Lanesborough. Jamie Wynne-Griffith timed his shots superbly, and hit the ball as hard as any boy at this level. Charlie Fletcher and Oliver Davies gave useful support in the top order.

George Quaile was the pick of the bowlers, his classic side-on action producing swing and lift to complement his accuracy. The reliable seam trio of Duncan MacFarlane, Andy Corridan and Andy Creed chipped in with vital wickets, as did Pickard and Davies. Charlie Russell-Jones, Charlie Court and Nick Pattinson offered great enthusiasm, while behind the stumps, Jonathon Buck improved with every game he played.

AVERAGES

BATSMAN	INNINGS	NOT OUT	RUNS	H. SCORE	AVERAGE
C. Pickard	12	3	410	107*	45.6
J. Wynne-Griffith	11	3	220	66*	27.5
O. Davies	10	1	190	41	21.1
C. Fletcher	10	1	126	37*	14.0

BOWLER	OVERS	MAIDENS	RUNS	WICKETS	AVERAGE
A. Creed	27	2	97	10	9.7
O. Davies	44	10	157	11	14.3
D. MacFarlane	37	5	161	11	14.6
G. Quaile	48	9	184	12	15.3
A. Corridan	52	10	169	11	15.4
C. Pickard	43	1	206	10	20.6

WICKET-KEEPER	PLAYED	CAUGHT	STUMPED
J. Buck	11	4	2

NOTABLE BATTING PERFORMANCES

PLAYER	OPPOSITION	SCORE
C. Pickard	Lanesborough	107*
C. Pickard	St. Andrew's Woking	77*
J. Wynne-Griffith	St. Andrew's Woking	66*
C. Pickard	Edgeborough	62

NOTABLE BOWLING PERFORMANCES

PLAYER	OPPOSITION	FIGURES
G. Quaile	The Ridge (South Africa)	4-30
A. Creed	Hoe Bridge	3-10
D. MacFarlane	Edgeborough	3-13
G. Quaile	King's College Wimbledon	3-7
D. MacFarlane	Millfield	3-18

ALDWICKBURY

Wheathampstead Road, Harpenden, Hertfordshire AL5 1AE

Tel: 01582 713022 Fax: 01582 767696

Email: secretary@aldwickbury.org.uk

Headmaster: V.W. Hales Master i/c Cricket: R.A. Evans

2005 SEASON

Played: 4 Won: 1 Lost: 1 Drawn: 2

Captain: A.C. Spencer Vice-captain: A.M. Fahrenheim

Team selected from: S. Boothby, S. Collings, T. Cottrell,
C. Davies, A. Fahrenheim*, K. Fitzpatrick, R. Griffiths,
F. Hickson, S. Jackson, J. Latham, A. Spencer*, E. Tweddle.

SUMMARY

This season we had three matches rained off without a ball being bowled. Many of our practice sessions were severely curtailed by rain and one of our drawn matches started late because of heavy showers. Three other schools on our circuit could not arrange fixtures due to a full calendar.

Nevertheless, the boys were very keen and worked hard to improve their skills. In our first three matches we never lost more than four wickets, so the majority of the team had limited opportunities to impress with the bat. However, we used between six and eight bowlers in every game so every boy was at least involved.

Captain Alex Spencer is an outstanding wicket-keeper/batsman and he was our leading run-scorer. Andrew Fahrenheim showed excellent potential with the bat. Sam Boothby, James Latham and Rhys Griffiths all had their moments and are exciting prospects for next year. The games we did manage to play were all very competitive and enjoyable, even the only limited over game we played, when an opposing batsman played a superb match winning innings of 136*.

AVERAGES

BATSMAN	INNINGS	NOT OUT	RUNS	H. SCORE	AVERAGE
A. Spencer	4	3	174	75*	174.0
J. Latham	2	1	68	56*	68.0
A. Fahrenheim	4	0	62	30	15.5
R. Griffiths	4	0	50	16	12.5

BOWLER	OVERS	MAIDENS	RUNS	WICKETS	AVERAGE
S. Boothby	24	2	54	6	9.0
T. Cottrell	15	3	41	3	13.7
J. Latham	28	5	99	7	14.1

WICKET-KEEPER	PLAYED	CAUGHT	STUMPED
A. Spencer	4	1	1

NOTABLE BATTING PERFORMANCES

PLAYER	OPPOSITION	SCORE
A. Spencer	The Beacon	75*
A. Spencer	York House	69*
A. Spencer	Orley Farm	26*
A. Fahrenheim	St. Martin's	30
J. Latham	St. Martin's	56*

NOTABLE BOWLING PERFORMANCES

PLAYER	OPPOSITION	FIGURES
S. Boothby	St. Martin's	8-2-19-5
S. Boothby	The Beacon	8-0-16-1
E. Tweddle	The Beacon	6-0-14-2
J. Latham	Orley Farm	8-1-25-2
J. Latham	York House	6-1-24-2
J. Latham	St. Martin's	7-2-21-2
T. Cottrell	St. Martin's	5-2-12-2

ASHDOWN HOUSE

Forest Row, East Sussex RH18 5JY

Tel: 01342 822574 Fax: 01342 824380

Email: secretary@ashdownhouse.com

Headmaster: R. Taylor Master i/c Cricket: D. Reavill

2005 SEASON

Played: 17 Won: 6 Lost: 5 Drawn: 5 Tied: 1

Captain: H. Hely-Hutchinson Vice-captain: A. Hill

Team selected from: H. Hely-Hutchinson*, R. Hovey*,
J. Richardson*, M. Haddock*, N. Hely-Hutchinson*, A. Hill*,
F. Cripps, A. Beale, N. Roope, T. Evans, M. Turner,
P. Egerton-Warburton, G. Talbot, C. Haddock, H. Rogers,
M. Coles, G. Hurd, M. Emlyn-Williams, E. Stogdale.
Scorer: W. Koops

SUMMARY

The 1st XI had a tremendous season with plenty of memorable moments. The biggest highlight of all was playing 17 matches and only having one boring draw when, despite massive temptation and generous offerings, the opposition still refused to try and chase. It was unbelievably heartwarming that every player in the team understood the concept of cricket and enjoyed playing properly.

Our team highlights were the victories over Vinehall, Windlesham, Yardley Court and St. Bede's. There were lessons learnt when three teams were left 9 wickets down and throughout the season we had a constant desire to bat first.

Individually, Richardson's and Haddock's runs were always very impressive and Hill's bowling was wonderful to watch - only 1 wicket in his last five games shows that spinners can prosper early season. Nick Hely-Hutchinson's assaults were a joy to witness. Nothing can top the tie against The Dragon, during our tour, when Hovey knocked over the off-stump in the final over of the match. In the last match of the season, when 316 runs were scored against Brambletye, the captain took 8 wickets with typically delightful leg-spin.

AVERAGES

BATSMAN	INNINGS	NOT OUT	RUNS	H. SCORE	AVERAGE
J. Richardson	17	4	475	77	36.5
T. Evans	6	5	31	11*	31.0
M. Haddock	17	0	447	140	26.3
A. Beale	9	2	173	65*	24.7
F. Cripps	8	0	178	57	22.3
N. Hely-Hutchinson	16	1	308	69	20.5

BOWLER	OVERS	MAIDENS	RUNS	WICKETS	AVERAGE
F. Cripps	6.0	0	21	5	4.2
H. Hely-Hutchinson	13.3	4	57	8	7.1
M. Haddock	81.4	16	226	21	10.8
M. Turner	26.0	9	90	8	11.2
A. Hill	141.0	29	427	32	13.3
R. Hovey	90.3	19	346	23	15.0

WICKET-KEEPER	PLAYED	CAUGHT	STUMPED
N. Roope	9	3	1
C. Haddock	6	1	3

NOTABLE BATTING PERFORMANCES

PLAYER	OPPOSITION	SCORE
M. Haddock	Brambletye	140
J. Richardson	Brambletye	77
N. Hely-Hutchinson	Vinehall	69
A. Beale	Cumnor House	65*
N. Hely-Hutchinson	Winchester House	63*
J. Richardson	Cumnor House	62
M. Haddock	Cottesmore	60

NOTABLE BOWLING PERFORMANCES

PLAYER	OPPOSITION	FIGURES
H. Hely-Hutchinson	Brambletye	10-3-47-8
A. Hill	Wellesley House	12-1-39-7
M. Turner	St. Bede's	9-6-9-4
R. Hovey	Great Walstead	8-3-9-4
A. Hill	Windlesham	5-2-11-4
M. Haddock	Vinehall	8-3-15-4
R. Hovey	The Dragon	7.1-0-20-4

BARNARDISTON HALL

Barnardiston, Nr. Haverhill, Suffolk CB9 7TG
Tel: 01440 786316 Fax: 01440 786355
Email: enquiries@barnardiston-hall.co.uk
Headmaster: Col. K.A. Boulter Master i/c Cricket: Nick Willings

2005 SEASON

Played: 16   Won: 9   Lost: 5   Drawn: 2

Captain: C. McGladdery   Vice-captain: J. Wentworth-James

Team selected from: C. McGladdery, J. Wentworth-James,
J. Harris, C. Gregory, A. Bibby, H. Bravery, H. King, J. Clifton,
J. Wilkinson, A. Davidson, F. Preston, T. Atkins, T. Bright.

Scorer: A. Chung

SUMMARY

Barnardiston Hall is a small Suffolk school and this season's results have been excellent considering its size and the talent available. The school retained the Borders League Trophy, did well in the domestic matches and went on tour, playing against St. John's-on-the-Hill, Beaudesert Park and Pinewood. We won against St. John's-on-the-Hill, lost to Beaudesert Park and had an excellent draw with Pinewood (BHPS 183-8 and Pinewood 137-8).

Charles McGladdery, the captain, hit a splendid 110* versus South Lee where the school scored 268-1. John Wentworth-James scored four fifties, kept wicket and bowled slow left arm on occasions. Josh Harris was the other main batsman and Jack Clifton was the pick of the bowlers. The bowling was our weakest suit and his five wickets against St. John's-on-the-Hill was due reward.

AVERAGES

BATSMAN	INNINGS	NOT OUT	RUNS	H. SCORE	AVERAGE
J. Harris	16	6	348	66*	34.8
C. McGladdery	16	2	460	110*	32.9
J. Wentworth-James	15	1	388	82	27.7
F. Preston	7	1	149	41*	24.8

BOWLER	OVERS	MAIDENS	RUNS	WICKETS	AVERAGE
J. Clifton	66.2	8	258	23	11.2
J. Wilkinson	39.2	2	180	12	15.0
C. McGladdery	51.4	6	193	11	17.5
J. Harris	76.4	11	274	15	18.3

WICKET-KEEPER	PLAYED	CAUGHT	STUMPED
J. Wentworth-James	15	7	4

NOTABLE BATTING PERFORMANCES

PLAYER	OPPOSITION	SCORE
C. McGladdery	South Lee	110*
C. McGladdery	Holmwood House	67
J. Wentworth-James	South Lee	82
J. Wentworth-James	Royal Hospital	58
J. Wentworth-James	Moreton Hall	52*
J. Harris	South Lee	66*
J. Harris	Helions Bumpstead	53*

NOTABLE BOWLING PERFORMANCES

PLAYER	OPPOSITION	FIGURES
J. Clifton	St. John's-on-the-Hill	5-30
J. Wilkinson	Brockley	3-9

BEAUDESERT PARK

Minchinhampton, Gloucestershire GL6 9AF

Tel: 01453 832072 Fax: 01453 836040

Email: office@beaudesert.gloucs.sch.uk

Headmaster: J.P.R. Womersley Master i/c Cricket: S.T.P. O'Malley

2005 SEASON

Played: 15   Won: 9   Lost: 3   Drawn: 3

Captain: J. Priest

Team selected from: E. Arbuthnott*, S. Browne*, T. Dauncey*, F. Garner, B. Hayward, E. Jewell, F. Miles, G. Mitchell, T. Morley, J. Priest*, M. Radford*, F. Sowerbutts*, T. Wyld*,W. Warner.

SUMMARY

The three losses, against Summer Fields (Twenty20), Kwazulu Natal and Clifton, were offset by excellent cricket throughout the rest of the season, notably versus Dean Close, Cheltenham and St. Hugh's. The most exciting game was undoubtedly against Pinewood. Five overs into our innings, chasing a modest 64, and with the score on 8-4, winning seemed a distant prospect. On 37-8 it appeared impossible. However, stoic batting from M. Radford (24*) saved the day with one wicket in hand. Beating last year's unbeaten XI by one wicket was a highlight, as was the bowling and fielding performance against Kwazulu Natal.

The side was intelligently captained by Priest and he, Sowerbutts, Dauncey and Morley formed a strong bowling attack. Apart from the successful chase of 110 (for the loss of only 3 wickets) versus Cheltenham, batting second was rarely comfortable. Batting first was solid and any fragility was covered by one of several stepping into the breach. Arbuthnott and Wyld played sensibly, and the team always posted decent totals. A memorable season.

AVERAGES

BATSMAN	INNINGS	NOT OUT	RUNS	H. SCORE	AVERAGE
F. Sowerbutts	14	2	353	87	29.4
T. Wyld	9	2	179	38	25.6
J. Priest	12	2	222	62*	22.2
M. Radford	12	4	153	35*	19.1

BOWLER	OVERS	MAIDENS	RUNS	WICKETS	AVERAGE
F. Sowerbutts	77	26	192	25	7.7
J. Priest	77	19	210	24	8.8
T. Morley	51.4	9	170	16	10.6
T. Dauncey	87.4	10	281	25	11.2

WICKET-KEEPER	PLAYED	CAUGHT	STUMPED
S. Browne	14	3	11

NOTABLE BATTING PERFORMANCES

PLAYER	OPPOSITION	SCORE
F. Sowerbutts	Dean Close	87
F. Sowerbutts	Barnardiston Hall	57
J. Priest	Barnardiston Hall	62*
E. Arbuthnott	St. Hugh's	41
T. Wyld	St. Hugh's	38
M. Radford	Prior Park	35*

NOTABLE BOWLING PERFORMANCES

PLAYER	OPPOSITION	FIGURES
T. Dauncey	St. Hugh's	10.2-2-25-5
J. Priest	Barnardiston Hall	7-2-20-5
T. Dauncey	Pinewood	6-1-12-5
F. Sowerbutts	St. John's	7-1-19-4
T. Dauncey	Clifton College	10-1-43-4
J. Priest	Cheltenham College	8-4-13-3
T. Dauncey	Kwazulu (South Africa)	11-1-37-3

BEESTON HALL

West Runton, Cromer, Norfolk NR27 9NQ

Tel: 01263 837324 Fax: 01263 838177

Email: office@beestonhall.co.uk

Headmaster: I.K. MacAskill Master i/c Cricket: A. Richards

2005 SEASON

Played: 15   Won: 8   Lost: 4   Drawn: 3

Captain: G. Lake   Vice-captain: A. Innes

Team selected from: G. Lake*, A. Innes*, T. Bacon,
W. Agnew, H. Ruffell, W. O'Connell, O. Middleditch,
J. Cubitt, T. Cross, B. Fox, A. Chance, G. Cushing,
C. Wilson, F. Heathcote, H. Ripley.

Scorer: I. Scott-Moncrieff

SUMMARY

In a rather damp season, we were lucky to only lose two matches to the weather. It was only after the end of term at the Caldicott Cricket Festival that we experienced some glorious sunny days and up to that point we had not drawn a match!

The team had no outstanding individuals but played with great enthusiasm. They won some very exciting games and when they failed, they failed in catastrophic ways. On no less than five occasions we were two wickets down with less than 10 runs on the board. However, the team won two of these matches!

Highlights of the season were the matches at the Caldicott Festival played on superb pitches against good sides and the game against Norwich School, which swung every way and was decided in the final over. We look forward to another good season next year with many promising players returning.

AVERAGES

BATSMAN	INNINGS	NOT OUT	RUNS	H. SCORE	AVERAGE
H. Ruffell	12	1	210	55	19.1
B. Fox	14	5	167	28	18.6
O. Middleditch	10	3	114	49	16.3
G. Lake	14	1	182	40	14.0
A. Innes	14	1	177	64	13.6
W. O'Connell	12	1	133	34	12.1

BOWLER	OVERS	MAIDENS	RUNS	WICKETS	AVERAGE
O. Middleditch	33.1	4	94	16	5.9
W. Agnew	66.5	8	238	18	13.2
T. Bacon	62.4	16	207	15	13.8
H. Ruffell	57	10	201	14	14.4
A. Chance	40	5	180	10	18.0
W. O'Connell	37.4	3	135	7	19.3

WICKET-KEEPER	PLAYED	CAUGHT	STUMPED
T. Cross	11	2	1
G. Cushing	4	4	-

NOTABLE BATTING PERFORMANCES

PLAYER	OPPOSITION	SCORE
A. Innes	Caldicott	64
H. Ruffell	Town Close	55
G. Lake	Haileybury	40
O. Middleditch	Sussex House	49

NOTABLE BOWLING PERFORMANCES

PLAYER	OPPOSITION	FIGURES
O. Middleditch	Norwich	5.2-3-12-4
W. Agnew	Merchiston Castle	8-0-25-4
O. Middleditch	Old Buckenham	1.2-0-1-3

BELHAVEN HILL

Dunbar, East Lothian EH42 1NN
Tel: 01368 862785 Fax: 01368 865225
Email: headmaster@belhavenhill.com

Headmaster: M. Osborne Master i/c Cricket: W. Townshend

2005 SEASON

Played: 4   Won: 2   Lost: 1   Drawn: 1

Captain: T. Greville-Williams

Team selected from: T. Greville-Williams*, H. Dalrymple,
F. Coleman*, S. Heward, R. Baynes, H. Rogers, W. Ayles,
F. Leeming, W. Stewart, H. Carnegie, A. Kelly.

SUMMARY

This was an exceptionally diappointing season for the 1st XI. A
single case of mumps led to the first three fixtures being
cancelled. A further two were lost to rain and another when the
opposition failed to honour the fixture.

Nevertheless the boys continued to practise hard and showed
remarkable enthusiasm for the game. They won the matches
against Merchiston Castle and then Loretto and were in a
dominant position after posting 200 against Bramcote, but were
unable to pick up the last two wickets.

The side retained the trophy for the Glenalmond six-a-side
competition, winning a gripping final. F. Coleman, T. Greville-
Williams and H. Rogers were chosen to play for the East of
Scotland and F. Coleman went on to play for Scotland.

NOTABLE BATTING PERFORMANCES

PLAYER	OPPOSITION	SCORE
F. Coleman	Merchiston Castle	60
T. Greville-Williams	Bramcote	72*

NOTABLE BOWLING PERFORMANCES

PLAYER	OPPOSITION	FIGURES
F. Coleman	Merchiston Castle	8-2-12-3
T. Greville-Williams	Merchiston Castle	8-2-13-3
H. Rogers	Loretto	4-0-14-3

The Preparatory Schools' Cricket Almanac

"WANTS YOU"

Please spread the word by encouraging other preparatory schools to contact us for inclusion in next year's edition

The Editors, PSCA, 2 Malvern Cottages, Stowe Lane, Colwall, Nr Malvern, Worcs. WR13 6EH
Tel 01684 541167 Tel/fax 01684 833578
psca@wisteriabooks.co.uk   www.wisteriabooks.co.uk

BICKLEY PARK

24 Page Heath Lane, Bickley, Kent BR1 2DS
Tel: 020 8467 2195 Fax: 020 8325 5511
Email: info@bickleyparkschool.co.uk
Headmaster: P. Ashley   Master i/c Cricket: A. Hyslop

2005 SEASON

Played: 9 Won: 5   Lost: 4

Captain: N. Worsley Vice-captain: T. Howarth

Team selected from: N. Worsley*, T. Howarth*, J. Henry*, A. Hayward, E. Whyte, J. Hamel, S. Jackson, O. Robinson, M. Faulder, C. Edwards, C. Bowdler, M. Davison, A. Jones.

Scorer: B. Stanley

SUMMARY

After a couple of early washouts, we began our season with disappointing performances against DCPS and Thomas's Clapham. Chasing only 97 to win after an outstanding spell of bowling by Thomas Howarth (5-7), we collapsed to 85 all out. After this set back, we were much improved. Excellent victories were gained against Colfe's, St. Dunstan's, King's Rochester, St. Aubyn's and the Fathers XI.

The result of the season was undoubtedly against King's Rochester. Chasing a challenging total, and after the loss of early wickets, Jack Henry played an outstanding innings with a display of 'savage' hitting on his way to 60*.

Nicholas Worsley led the team very well and contributed consistently with both bat and ball.

AVERAGES

BATSMAN	INNINGS	NOT OUT	RUNS	H. SCORE	AVERAGE
J. Henry	6	2	117	60*	29.3
A. Hayward	5	2	75	60*	25.0
N. Worsley	9	0	175	54	19.4
C. Bowdler	9	1	121	37*	15.1
J. Howarth	6	0	85	33	14.2

BOWLER	OVERS	MAIDENS	RUNS	WICKETS	AVERAGE
J. Henry	18	4	31	6	5.2
T. Howarth	30	3	124	10	12.4
N. Worsley	43.1	4	164	10	16.4
E. Whyte	27	0	131	8	16.4
C. Edwards	22.2	3	111	5	22.2
O. Robinson	20	2	91	4	22.8

WICKET-KEEPER	PLAYED	CAUGHT	STUMPED
J. Hamel	8	3	0
M. Davison	1	0	0

NOTABLE BATTING PERFORMANCES

PLAYER	OPPOSITION	SCORE
N. Worsley	St. Dunstan's	50
N. Worsley	Dulwich College	54
A. Hayward	St. Aubyn's	60*
J. Henry	King's Rochester	60*
C. Bowdler	St. Aubyn's	37*

NOTABLE BOWLING PERFORMANCES

PLAYER	OPPOSITION	FIGURES
T. Howarth	Thomas's Clapham	5-7
N. Worsley	Colfe's	3-6
J. Henry	St. Dunstan's	2-0

BIRCHFIELD

Harriot Hayes Lane, Albrighton, Wolverhampton WV7 3AF

Tel: 01902 372534 Fax: 01902 373516
Email: office@birchfieldschool.co.uk

Headmaster: R. Merriman   Master i/c Cricket: Rob Newey

2005 SEASON

Played: 8   Won: 1   Lost: 4   Drawn: 3

Captain: T. Bozman   Vice-captain: A. Wake

Team selected from: T. Bozman*, A. Wake, J. Drumm-Roberts,
H. Dawson, R. Smith, J. Nicholls, M. Johnson, D. Rajput,
J. Lazzeri, A. Green, C. Whittle, M. Young.

SUMMARY

A difficult season, although there were some good individual
performances. The highlight was a determined fighting draw
with Foremarke, followed the next day by finishing runners-up
at the Wrekin six-a-side tournament. The best performance of
the season was saved for the JET cup against Packwood.

The captain, Thomas Bozman, represented the county U13
team and Henry Dawson the U12.

Did you know? . . . The first Test match took place
between England and Australia in 1877 at Melbourne.
Australia won by 45 runs in front of a crowd that at one
time reached 12,000. The Ashes legend was not born
until five years later when in 1882 Australia beat a full
England side in England for the first time.

AVERAGES

BATSMAN	INNINGS	NOT OUT	RUNS	H. SCORE	AVERAGE
A. Wake	8	3	135	38*	27.0
T. Bozman	8	2	132	50*	22.0
J. Drumm-Roberts	8	1	135	64	19.3

BOWLER	OVERS	MAIDENS	RUNS	WICKETS	AVERAGE
A. Wake	54	3	305	13	23.5
T. Bozman	48	1	165	4	41.3
H. Dawson	48	0	285	5	57.0

WICKET-KEEPER	PLAYED	CAUGHT	STUMPED
J. Drumm-Roberts	8	1	4

NOTABLE BATTING PERFORMANCES

PLAYER	OPPOSITION	SCORE
T. Bozman	Packwood Haugh	50*
J. Drumm-Roberts	Denstone	64

NOTABLE BOWLING PERFORMANCES

PLAYER	OPPOSITION	FIGURES
A. Wake	Pinewood	4-18
H. Dawson	Pinewood	2-11
A. Wake	Abberley Hall	2-39
J. Lazzeri	Kingsland Grange	3-19

BISHOPSGATE

Bishopsgate Road, Englefield Green, Egham, Surrey TW20 0YJ

Tel: 01784 432109 Fax: 01784 430460

Email: office@bishopsgate.surrey.sch.uk

Headmaster: M. Dunning   Master i/c Cricket: N. Harman

2005 SEASON

Played: 6   Won: 1   Lost: 4   Drawn: 1

Captain: M. Dunn   Vice-captain: J. Wagner

Team selected from: N. Bahlsen, E. Croasdale, M. Curran,
S. Davies*, R. Dobson*, M. Dunn*, A. Goodman,
N. Henderson-Williams*, D. Johnson*, M. Lee, A. Leoni-Sceti,
W. Michele*, S. Osborne*, K. Raslan, J. Wagner*, S. Mohsen.

SUMMARY

The standard of cricket throughout Bishopsgate has improved dramatically this season and has been exemplified by the 1st XI's performances. Unfortunately this is not evident from the statistics. Had the toss of the coin worked in our favour more often, several results could have been reversed.

After a damp April, our season got off to the perfect start with victory in a low scoring match against Hoe Bridge on a rain-sodden pitch. The highlight of the game was undoubtedly a magnificent bowling performance from our captain Matthew Dunn. He captained a side with a healthy mix of U12 and U13 players, five of whom were in their second season for the 1st XI. He led the side by example, contributing well in every game with both bat and ball. Will Michele also rediscovered good form with the bat with several brief, but dramatic, attacking displays.

The season in general was compiled of a series of very tightly contested games, with the final twist continually working in favour of the opposition, despite some breathtaking performances by the Bishopsgate team.

AVERAGES

BATSMAN	INNINGS	NOT OUT	RUNS	H. SCORE	AVERAGE
M. Dunn	5	0	129	38	25.8
W. Michele	5	0	69	22	13.8
N. Henderson-Williams	4	1	27	24*	9.0
A. Goodman	4	0	34	12	8.5
S. Davies	5	1	33	20*	8.3
J. Wagner	5	2	21	11*	7.0

BOWLER	OVERS	MAIDENS	RUNS	WICKETS	AVERAGE
M. Dunn	29.1	3	126	12	10.5
J. Wagner	27.5	3	127	8	15.9
S. Osborne	7	0	48	3	16.0
M. Lee	14	1	45	2	22.5
A. Goodman	13	1	77	2	38.5

WICKET-KEEPER	PLAYED	CAUGHT	STUMPED
A. Leoni-Sceti	4	0	0
K. Raslan	2	0	0

NOTABLE BATTING PERFORMANCES

PLAYER	OPPOSITION	SCORE
M. Dunn	Sunningdale	38
M. Dunn	St. George's Windsor	35
M. Dunn	Hoe Bridge	29
N. Henderson-Williams	Fathers	24*
W. Michele	Fathers	22
S. Davies	Twickenham	20*
W. Michele	Sunningdale	20

NOTABLE BOWLING PERFORMANCES

PLAYER	OPPOSITION	FIGURES
M. Dunn	Hoe Bridge	5-33
M. Dunn	St. George's Windsor	3-15
J. Wagner	Fathers	3-20
M. Lee	St. George's Windsor	2-12
A. Goodman	Twickenham	2-21
S. Osborne	Fathers	2-21
J. Wagner	St. George's Windsor	2-34

BRAMCOTE

Filey Road, Scarborough, Yorkshire YO11 2TT

Tel: 01723 373086 Fax: 01723 364186

Email: office@bramcoteschool.com

Headmaster: A.G.W. Lewin   Master i/c Cricket: Andrew Snow

2005 SEASON

Played: 9   Won: 2   Lost: 2   Drawn: 5

Captain: R. McKenzie   Vice-captain: O. Gibbons

Team selected from: R. McKenzie*, O. Gibbons*, J. Armour*, S. Forbes, F. Smyth, N. Robinson, C. Robinson, O. Newby, H. Iles, H. Forbes, R. Sword, C. Lacey, P. Gonzales.

SUMMARY

The Bramcote XI had a good season. Two early victories were encouraging but these were balanced by two defeats later in the term. The loss of the captain's bowling for many matches was crucial and as a result several games were drawn.

Raffan McKenzie played the best innings in an exciting game at Aysgarth. Fred Smyth has another year to play in the XI and showed promise as an opener. Some of our other batsmen failed to fulfil their potential.

Oliver Gibbons bowled his leg-spin with real enthusiasm but with only two five wicket hauls did not cause as much damage as we had hoped. Oliver Newby showed promise for the future, already turning the ball a long way. As with the batting, the bowling was far too ordinary in the main.

In difficult circumstances the boys maintained a good team spirit and the side never gave up without a fight.

AVERAGES

BATSMAN	INNINGS	NOT OUT	RUNS	H. SCORE	AVERAGE
H. Forbes	5	4	35	16*	35.0
F. Smyth	8	2	163	48*	27.2
R. McKenzie	6	1	133	68	26.6
J. Armour	7	2	126	37*	25.2
S. Forbes	8	1	107	52	15.3
O. Gibbons	5	0	48	25	9.6

BOWLER	OVERS	MAIDENS	RUNS	WICKETS	AVERAGE
O. Gibbons	81.2	4	365	19	19.2
H. Forbes	9	3	40	2	20.0
R. McKenzie	28	5	81	4	20.2
O. Newby	39	2	165	8	20.6
J. Armour	60.4	6	260	12	21.7
H. Iles	48	4	179	7	25.6

WICKET-KEEPER	PLAYED	CAUGHT	STUMPED
N. Robinson	9	1	3

NOTABLE BATTING PERFORMANCES

PLAYER	OPPOSITION	SCORE
R. McKenzie	Aysgarth	68
S. Forbes	Woodleigh	52
F. Smyth	Aysgarth	48*
F. Smyth	Woodleigh	48

NOTABLE BOWLING PERFORMANCES

PLAYER	OPPOSITION	FIGURES
O. Gibbons	Scarborough College	6-20
O. Gibbons	Woodleigh	5-13
O. Newby	Belhaven Hill	4-28
J. Armour	Terrington Hall	4-15

BRANDESTON HALL

Brandeston, Nr. Woodbridge, Suffolk IP13 7AH

Tel: 01728 685331 Fax: 01728 685561

Email: office@brandestonhall.co.uk

Headmaster: J. Kelsall Master i/c Cricket: C. Reynell

2005 SEASON

Played: 8 Won: 3 Lost: 1 Drawn: 4

Captain: H. Wrinch Vice-captain: C. Treacey

Team selected from: H. Wrinch*, R. Gear*, H. Stewart, C. Treacey*, C. O'Leary, A. Dunham, W. Nias, L. Scott, B. Elliott, J. Simpson, L. Buckingham*.

SUMMARY

It was always felt that much of our success this summer would hinge on the elegant strokeplay of left-handed skipper Harry Wrinch. He took the first of his 23 wickets and scored a wonderful 59* in the victory over a strong Felsted side. In the bitter conditions of early May the team struggled in the field, but were rallied by resolute batting from tailenders Scott, Simpson and Dunham. This was mirrored by Connor O'Leary at the top of the order and, as the wickets became harder, Robert Gear came into form with his destructive batting. He was ably supported by our keeper/batsman Chris Treacey who had an excellent season behind the stumps.

In the bowling department, Lee Buckingham bowled with fire and James Simpson, one of only two Year 7 boys in the side, showed unerring accuracy. The record of three wins and four draws says much about the boys' character and determination, as well as their unwillingness to accept defeat.

As the season drew to a close with the seventh Brandeston Hall Cricket Festival, it became evident that the boys had grown into a real cricket 'team'.

AVERAGES

BATSMAN	INNINGS	NOT OUT	RUNS	H. SCORE	AVERAGE
H. Wrinch	8	3	157	59*	31.4
R. Gear	8	0	147	59	18.4

BOWLER	OVERS	MAIDENS	RUNS	WICKETS	AVERAGE
H. Wrinch	74.2	6	300	23	13.0
J. Simpson	57.4	8	198	15	13.2
L. Scott	32	4	130	7	18.6
L. Buckingham	51	4	198	8	24.7
A. Dunham	8	0	50	2	25.0

WICKET-KEEPER	PLAYED	CAUGHT	STUMPED
C. Treacey	8	8	3

NOTABLE BATTING PERFORMANCES

PLAYER	OPPOSITION	SCORE
R. Gear	Felsted	49
H. Wrinch	Felsted	59*
R. Gear	Town Close	59
H. Wrinch	Holmwood House	40*

NOTABLE BOWLING PERFORMANCES

PLAYER	OPPOSITION	FIGURES
H. Wrinch	Felsted	4-0-10-3
H. Wrinch	Ipswich	10-0-32-4
L. Buckingham	Town Close	8-3-16-4
H. Wrinch	Gresham's	7-0-34-3
L. Scott	Town Close	6-1-19-3
J. Simpson	Holmwood House	7.4-1-28-3
H. Wrinch	Holmwood House	12-2-35-5

CALDICOTT

Crown Lane, Farnham Royal, Berkshire SL2 3SL

Tel: 01753 649300 Fax: 01753 649325

Email: office@caldicott.com

Headmaster: S. Doggart   Master i/c Cricket: K. Rich

2005 SEASON

Played: 15   Won: 2   Lost: 3   Drawn: 10

Captain: J. Gray   Vice-captain: C. Wakefield

Team selected from: J. Gray, C. Wakefield*, G. Dashwood*, F. Cowdrey*, T. Bates*, A. Purewal, A. Nimba, J. Cowdrey, A. Bone, N. Allred, H. Swift, W. Finley.

Scorer: J. Taylor

SUMMARY

The highlight of a rather frustrating season was the batting of the top order. Fabian Cowdrey, in particular, amassed a huge aggregate of runs, with another season left. He scored back-to-back hundreds early season and was devastating once he had settled in. Chris Wakefield and Tom Bates were also consistent, and when batting first we often scored big totals in quick time.

To a certain extent the pitch at Caldicott was too good. Once teams were determined not to get bowled out, we lacked the killer instinct on such a true pitch to earn the victory. The number of draws was very disappointing. We always played attacking cricket, but despite finding ourselves in winning positions in nine matches, we could not bowl teams out. George Dashwood took time to recapture his form of last season but bowled beautiful off-spin in the second half of term. Julius Cowdrey bowled excellent left-arm orthodox and Alastair Bone produced some unplayable leg-breaks. There was much good cricket played this season, but we were left to reflect on some rather indifferent catching and a lack of quality seam bowling.

AVERAGES

BATSMAN	INNINGS	NOT OUT	RUNS	H. SCORE	AVERAGE
F. Cowdrey	15	2	735	134	56.5
C. Wakefield	14	2	471	114*	39.3
T. Bates	14	1	357	74*	27.5
G. Dashwood	12	4	184	48	23.0

BOWLER	OVERS	MAIDENS	RUNS	WICKETS	AVERAGE
A. Bone	67	11	233	17	13.7
J. Cowdrey	96	17	272	18	15.1
F. Cowdrey	78	11	294	19	15.5
G. Dashwood	168	23	587	29	20.2

WICKET-KEEPER	PLAYED	CAUGHT	STUMPED
C. Wakefield	14	6	5

NOTABLE BATTING PERFORMANCES

PLAYER	OPPOSITION	SCORE
F. Cowdrey	Papplewick	125*
F. Cowdrey	The Dragon	134
C. Wakefield	Elstree	114*
C. Wakefield	Merchiston Castle	110*
F. Cowdrey	St. John's Northwood	94
F. Cowdrey	Beeston Hall	91*
T. Bates	Papplewick	74*

NOTABLE BOWLING PERFORMANCES

PLAYER	OPPOSITION	FIGURES
G. Dashwood	Merchiston Castle	13-4-24-5
J. Cowdrey	Papplewick	7-0-14-4
F. Cowdrey	St. John's Beaumont	10-1-29-4
G. Dashwood	The Dragon	10-0-37-4
G. Dashwood	Cothill	14-3-34-4
J. Cowdrey	Elstree	10-0-49-4

CHAFYN GROVE

Bourne Avenue, Salisbury, Wiltshire SP1 1LR
Tel: 01722 333423   Fax: 01722 323114
Email: officecgs@lineone.net
Headmaster: E. Newton   Master i/c Cricket: D. Renham

2005 SEASON

Played: 12   Won: 9   Lost: 1   Drawn: 2

Captain: T. Darby   Vice-captain: B. Peters

Team selected from: T. Darby*, A. Jones*, B. Stuchbury*, H. Cox*, B. Peters*, T. Loudon, R. Mann, R. Bennett, M. Leech, A. Leng, T. Poulton, J. Ballantyne-Dykes, O. Paine.

Scorer: Mrs F. Stuchbury

SUMMARY

The 1st XI had an excellent season, dominated by captain Thomas Darby whose batting was outstanding. A good team supported him, Alfie Jones impressing with the bat and Ben Stuchbury, our off-spinner, with the ball.

The only defeat, against Millfield in the JET cup quarter final, was disappointing as we were in a winning position at tea. The two draws were both 'winning draws' - one team 9 wickets down and the other 93 runs short, having played defensive cricket.

Thomas Darby

AVERAGES

BATSMAN	INNINGS	NOT OUT	RUNS	H. SCORE	AVERAGE
T. Darby	10	5	764	150*	152.8
A. Jones	10	4	196	53	32.7
H. Cox	7	2	140	63	28.0
R. Bennett	10	2	137	32	17.1
B. Stuchbury	8	2	79	36	13.2

BOWLER	OVERS	MAIDENS	RUNS	WICKETS	AVERAGE
T. Darby	52.3	14	119	25	4.8
B. Stuchbury	49.4	6	164	24	6.8
T. Loudon	30	4	79	10	7.9
B. Peters	58	8	204	17	12.0
R. Mann	34	6	130	9	14.4
A. Jones	36	2	119	7	17.0

WICKET-KEEPER	PLAYED	CAUGHT	STUMPED
H. Cox	10	6	2

NOTABLE BATTING PERFORMANCES

PLAYER	OPPOSITION	SCORE
T. Darby	Hazlegrove	150*
T. Darby	Sherborne	126*
T. Darby	Port Regis	132*
T. Darby	Dauntsey's	100*

CHELTENHAM COLLEGE

Thirlestaine Road, Cheltenham, Gloucestershire GL53 7AB

Tel: 01242 522697 Fax: 01242 265620
Email: parsley.kim@cheltcoll.gloucs.sch.uk

Headmaster: N.I. Archdale   Master i/c Cricket: K.A. Parsley

2005 SEASON

Played: 13   Won: 1   Lost: 10   Drawn: 2

Captain: H. Snell

Team selected from: P. Adams, R. Akingbehin, M. Arthur,
G. Barnett, H. Barthorp, H. Bristol, G. Edwards, J. Fletcher,
H. Jaggs, J. Mason, F. Nesbitt, C. Sault, G. Smith,
H. Snell*, C. Stuckey*.

SUMMARY

The season's record shows ten matches lost out of thirteen played - the most defeats in any single season. The opposition were never bowled out - this has happened only once in the last fifty-five years.

The reasons for these two statistics boil down to the basics in cricket. Inconsistencies in all three departments cost us dear throughout the thirteen fixtures, but above all it was an inability to bowl straight and to hold our catches that frequently let us down.

Did you know? . . . Of the last twenty-seven Tests at Lord's Australia have lost only once. The Oval, only a few miles away, is England's 'luckiest' home ground.

AVERAGES

BATSMAN	INNINGS	NOT OUT	RUNS	H. SCORE	AVERAGE
C. Stuckey	13	1	385	77*	32.1
H. Snell	13	4	125	36	13.9
G. Smith	12	1	150	32*	13.6
G. Barnett	12	1	146	35	13.3
J. Fletcher	6	4	24	12*	12.0
H. Barthorp	12	1	129	43*	11.7

BOWLER	OVERS	MAIDENS	RUNS	WICKETS	AVERAGE
H. Barthorp	62.1	11	222	14	15.8
J. Fletcher	42	5	175	10	17.5
H. Snell	76.2	15	258	12	21.5
H. Bristol	48.1	11	164	6	27.3
C. Stuckey	66	4	317	11	28.8

NOTABLE BATTING PERFORMANCES

PLAYER	OPPOSITION	SCORE
C. Stuckey	Wycliffe College	77*
C. Stuckey	Abberley Hall	70
C. Stuckey	The Dragon	60
C. Stuckey	Malsis	52
H. Barthorp	Dean Close	43*
H. Barthorp	Wycliffe College	40
H. Snell	City of London Freemen's	36

NOTABLE BOWLING PERFORMANCES

PLAYER	OPPOSITION	FIGURES
H. Barthorp	The Downs Wraxhall	3-13
J. Fletcher	The Dragon	3-21
H. Barthorp	Dean Close	3-23

CHRIST CHURCH CATHEDRAL

3 Brewer Street, Oxford, OX1 1QW

Tel: 01865 242561 Fax: 01865 202945
Email: schooloffice@cccs.org.uk

Headmaster: M. Bruce   Master i/c Cricket: P. Wavell

2005 SEASON

Played: 6   Won: 2   Lost: 4

Captain: P. Tyrer   Vice-captain: B. Etherton

Team selected from: P. Tyrer, R. Mynheer, B. Street, M. Knops, A. Smith, O. Ibru, A. Salvesen, D. Tyrer, J. Baker, G. Kambouroglou, B. Etherton, S. McDonnaugh.

SUMMARY

The team had a mixed season with pressure from injuries, other commitments and the weather. Three matches were completely washed out.

Paul Tyrer dominated the batting with some staunch assistance from Reuben Mynheer, but the bowling lacked penetration. As a young side, they should improve considerably by next season.

NOTABLE BATTING PERFORMANCES

PLAYER	OPPOSITION	SCORE
P. Tyrer	St. Hugh's	94*
P. Tyrer	Beachborough	58
R. Mynheer	Beachborough	18

NOTABLE BOWLING PERFORMANCES

PLAYER	OPPOSITION	FIGURES
D. Tyrer	Bruern Abbey	4-11
A. Smith	Beachborough	2-24

THE ARUNDEL CASTLE CRICKET FOUNDATION

by John Barclay
Director of Coaching and Cricket

With the notable exception of the country's independent schools, cricket has, for many years, been spread pretty thinly. It has scarcely played a major part in an education system where the world of sport has been deemed unimportant by successive governments since the war. In 1986 The Arundel Castle Cricket Foundation was formed in response to the urgent cry from teachers and children which demanded that something should be done to give a few more youngsters the chance to develop their lives through cricket. The main objective of the Foundation is to seek out the young, particularly those whose opportunities are limited, and bring them from unpromising environments – especially the inner cities – to Arundel for matches and coaching on the beautiful castle ground.

More than 200,000 boys and girls have played their part in the scheme, many of them with special needs and disabilities and most of them from challenging backgrounds. Cricket has, for them, proved itself to be a wonderful game for combining skills and good teamwork in a healthy educational environment. It has been hugely rewarding and great fun for all involved with the Arundel project, both to unearth the talent and to be the source of great pleasure which we hope will run with the youngsters as they grow up.

Funding has been tough. It always is. We battle to fund our projects and initiatives but, so far, have been loyally supported by people who believe, as we do, that creative sporting activity has a huge part to play in the development of the young and their spirit. Nothing could have helped us more than the inspiration derived from this summer's Ashes series. Cricket will, I believe, be seen in a new light which will hopefully spread through the length and breadth of the land.

John Barclay played first-class cricket from 1970-1986 scoring over 9000 runs and taking over 300 wickets. He was made captain of Sussex in 1981.

CLIFTON COLLEGE

The Avenue, Clifton, Bristol BS8 3HE

Tel: 0117 315 7502 Fax: 0117 315 7504

Email: LHall@clifton-college.avon.sch.uk

Headmaster: Dr R.J. Acheson   Master i/c Cricket: Lanion Hall

2005 SEASON

Played: 12   Won: 8   Drawn: 4

Captain: A. Moeller   Vice-captain: C. Walker

Team selected from: A. Moeller*, C. Walker*, C Walters, H. Greenbury, G. Nuttall, B. Figueiredo, M. Coveney, C. Brown, L. Hudson, S. Leech, G. Kinsey.

Scorer: M. Lidgitt

SUMMARY

Clifton College Prep has enjoyed one of its most successful and memorable cricket seasons. The 1st XI returned from a wonderful tour of South Africa, having played six matches against some of the best prep schools in Cape Town and East London, and the benefits were immediately obvious. The 1st XI's strength has been the all-round talent of the players and their enthusiasm to play exciting cricket.

The batting has been built around Charlie Walker, strongly supported by openers Andreas Moeller and Christian Walters, who gave our innings a positive start. Stroke-makers, Giles Nuttall and Harry Greenbury then followed. All the batsmen, Ben Figueiredo, Matthew Coveney, Sheridan Leech, George Kingsey, Chris Brown and Leo Hudson, played important innings during the season.

Our bowling attack was well balanced - pace from Chris Brown, Harry Greensbury, Leo Hudson and Matthew Coveney, followed by swing from Charlie Walker, Andreas Moeller, Ben Figueiredo and George Kinsey. Variation came from our off-spinner, Christian Walters, and leg-spinner, Giles Nuttall. The fielding has been very keen and at times outstanding.

AVERAGES

BATSMAN	INNINGS	NOT OUT	RUNS	H. SCORE	AVERAGE
C. Walker	11	2	550	79	61.1
G. Nuttall	9	2	212	39	30.3
C. Walters	12	3	214	54	23.8
A. Moeller	12	1	238	42	21.6
H. Greenbury	10	2	112	66*	14.0

BOWLER	OVERS	MAIDENS	RUNS	WICKETS	AVERAGE
H. Greenbury	53	18	92	14	6.6
G. Nuttall	34	5	79	9	8.8
C. Walters	50	10	164	18	9.1
C. Brown	60	17	122	12	10.2
C. Walker	68	21	203	19	10.7
A. Moeller	52	4	234	17	13.8

WICKET-KEEPER	PLAYED	CAUGHT	STUMPED
S. Leech	12	5	2

NOTABLE BATTING PERFORMANCES

PLAYER	OPPOSITION	SCORE
C. Walters	Dean Close	54
A. Moeller	Cheltenham College	42
H. Greenbury	Cheltenham College	66*
C. Walker	Prior Park	60
C. Walker	QE Hospital	63
C. Walker	Millfield	57
C. Walker	Beaudesert Park	79

NOTABLE BOWLING PERFORMANCES

PLAYER	OPPOSITION	FIGURES
C. Walters	Cheltenham College	5-2
C. Walters	Beaudesert Park	6-12
G. Nuttall	Prior Park	4-17
G. Nuttall	King's Hall	3-3
C. Brown	Dean Close	3-8
H. Greenbury	Prior Park	3-7
C. Walker	Clifton (South Africa)	5-40

COTHILL HOUSE

Cothill, Nr. Abingdon, Oxfordshire OX13 6JL

Tel: 01865 390800 Fax: 01865 390205

Email: jane@cothill.net

Headmaster: N. R. Brooks

Masters i/c Cricket: N. Compton-Burnett and E. Tenison

2005 SEASON

Played: 12   Won: 5   Lost: 1   Drawn: 6

Captain: O. Hext   Vice-captain: W. Eden

Team selected from: O. Hext*, W. Taylor*, N. Ramsay*,
A. Gibbs*, R. Trower, W. Eden*, D. Pratt, R. Grace, G. Green,
J. Ashton, M. Everton-Wallach.

Scorer: C. Waldron

SUMMARY

This was a vintage year for Cothill House. A very strong team
were well led by Oliver Hext and vice-captain William Eden.

At Horris Hill we were set a daunting 153 to win. At 15-3
we were in trouble but super batting from Nicholas Ramsay
(80) and good support from Bertie Trower (33) guided us home
in an exciting run-chase.

Strong batting from the top five ensured Ludgrove were set
a tough 150 to win. After 8 overs they were 8-6. Ramsay's
figures of 4-4-0-6 did not flatter him one bit.

Hext batted beautifully all season and the highlight was at
Radley when he scored 60*. I would not be surprised to hear of
many more innings of the same calibre for his new school in the
future. Set a challenging 151 to win, we timed our run-chase to
perfection. Taylor (39) and Grace (23*) supported the captain to
win by 9 wickets.

George Green rounded off a great season with 5-18 against
Cheltenham College and was supported by some excellent
fielding from William Eden and the rest of the team.

AVERAGES

BATSMAN	INNINGS	NOT OUT	RUNS	H. SCORE	AVERAGE
O. Hext	11	3	282	60*	35.3
N. Ramsay	11	3	236	80	29.5
A. Gibbs	7	3	94	43*	23.5
W. Taylor	9	1	154	50*	19.3
R. Grace	5	1	73	23*	18.3
J. Ashton	9	1	102	32*	12.8

BOWLER	OVERS	MAIDENS	RUNS	WICKETS	AVERAGE
G. Green	42	5	155	14	11.1
N. Ramsay	89	20	219	18	12.2
J. Ashton	37	5	129	9	14.3
A. Gibbs	77	16	223	15	14.9
D. Pratt	50	8	151	5	30.2
O. Hext	65	3	235	7	33.6

WICKET-KEEPER	PLAYED	CAUGHT	STUMPED
W. Taylor	12	8	0

NOTABLE BATTING PERFORMANCES

PLAYER	OPPOSITION	SCORE
N. Ramsay	Horris Hill	80
O. Hext	Radley	60*
O. Hext	Ludgrove	51*
W. Taylor	Elstree	50*
O. Hext	Abingdon	44*
O. Hext	Summer Fields	44
A. Gibbs	Sunningdale	43*

NOTABLE BOWLING PERFORMANCES

PLAYER	OPPOSITION	FIGURES
N. Ramsay	Ludgrove	6-2
G. Green	Cheltenham College	5-18
G. Green	Summer Fields	4-19
N. Ramsay	Summer Fields	3-16
N. Ramsay	Elstree	3-22
J. Ashton	Horris Hill	2-0
M. Everton-Wallach	Cheltenham College	2-5

COTTESMORE

Buchan Hill, Pease Pottage, West Sussex RH11 9AU

Tel: 01293 520648 Fax: 01293 614784
Email: schooloffice@cottesmoreschool.com

Headmaster: I.J. Tysoe   Master i/c Cricket: A. Walker

2005 SEASON

Played: 14   Won: 5   Lost: 4   Drawn: 5

Captain: A. Harvey   Vice-captain: W. Boyd

Team selected from: A. Harvey, W. Boyd, S. Beegan,
W. Bellamy, C. Eastwood, I. Erhardt, M. Evans, A. Low,
A. Proudlock, G. Russell, F. Stockden,
H. Threlfall, C. Walker-Simms.

SUMMARY

Despite a soggy start to the season, all our fixtures were fulfilled. However, the records don't quite tell the full story. Draws in the first three games could quite easily have been victories but for a few extra minutes. Defeats to Mowden and Westbourne were contested with extremely weak sides, owing to school trips, and the fixture against Ashdown was a limited overs affair, falling just short of their massive first innings total, with 5 wickets remaining. Brambletye were the best opposition we faced and they were worthy victors in our game with them late on in the season.

Rather than having one or two superstars in the XI, I was pleased to coach a team containing many good players, several of which stay with us next year. It promises to be a very exciting season, one to which I very much look forward.

AVERAGES

BATSMAN	INNINGS	NOT OUT	RUNS	H. SCORE	AVERAGE
A. Low	11	4	155	25	22.1
W. Boyd	11	4	138	29	19.7
A. Harvey	13	1	234	76	19.5
S. Beegan	13	3	153	48*	15.3
C. Eastwood	5	2	43	20*	14.3
W. Bellamy	13	1	146	43	12.2

BOWLER	OVERS	MAIDENS	RUNS	WICKETS	AVERAGE
H. Threlfall	38	6	121	13	9.3
A. Low	75	10	261	24	10.9
A. Harvey	75	12	208	18	11.6
C. Eastwood	54	4	201	15	13.4
M. Evans	56	4	232	14	16.6

WICKET-KEEPER	PLAYED	CAUGHT	STUMPED
W. Boyd	13	8	4

NOTABLE BATTING PERFORMANCES

PLAYER	OPPOSITION	SCORE
A. Harvey	Ashdown House	76
S. Beegan	Great Walstead	48*
A. Harvey	Windlesham	44
W. Bellamy	Windlesham	43
M. Evans	Ashdown House	38

NOTABLE BOWLING PERFORMANCES

PLAYER	OPPOSITION	FIGURES
A. Low	Dorset House	8-2-18-5
M. Evans	Windlesham	6-0-29-5
H. Threlfall	Great Walstead	4-1-6-4
M. Evans	Cumnor House	5-0-17-4

CRAIGCLOWAN

Edinburgh Road, Perth, PH2 8PS
Tel: 01738 626310 Fax: 01738 440349
Email: mbeale@btconnect.com
Headmaster: M. Beale Master i/c Cricket: C.S. McCarthy

2005 SEASON

Played: 5   Won: 4   Lost: 1

Captain: P. Ross   Vice-captain: F. Cox

Team selected from: J. Arnot, C. Black, M. Brown, R. Clark,
F. Cox, N. Farrar, M. Fenton, S. Fenton, D. Ferry,
C. MacLean, M. McKenzie, D. Meikle, B. Melville,
P. Ross, R. Watson.

SUMMARY

On paper this always looked like a good team and the boys
didn't disappoint. Ably led by Peter Ross and Freddie Cox, both
winning Scotland caps at U13 and U12 levels respectively, the
squad played with tremendous respect for each other both on
and off the field. With little or no square practice due to the
'wet stuff', it proved difficult to get the season off the ground.

Rain and contagious disease put paid to the first two
matches but the boys soon took out their frustration on Dollar, a
young Cargilfield side, Lathallan and Riley. Rain descended
once again, but in Musselburgh we found an oasis of sunlight
where Loretto awaited us. In what can only be described as a
'nailbiter', the boys sadly managed to grab defeat from the jaws
of victory to notch up the only loss of the season.

Glenalmond hosted us twice in a week for an indoor 'bash'
and, once again, for the sixes tournament. Having beaten
everyone in some style to reach the final, we ended the day as
tired runners-up.

Many thanks to Mr Dennis Rix, our groundsman and
weather guru, and to all parents who braved the elements.

AVERAGES

BATSMAN	INNINGS	NOT OUT	RUNS	H. SCORE	AVERAGE
P. Ross	4	1	103	58	34.3
D. Meikle	4	1	64	30*	21.3
N. Farrar	2	0	30	26	15.0
F. Cox	4	1	44	27	14.7
R. Watson	4	1	42	27*	14.0

BOWLER	OVERS	MAIDENS	RUNS	WICKETS	AVERAGE
R. Clark	4	-	2	3	0.7
P. Ross	19	-	43	10	4.3
N. Farrar	6	-	14	3	4.7
S. Fenton	5	-	16	3	5.3
F. Cox	19	-	51	9	5.7

WICKET-KEEPER	PLAYED	CAUGHT	STUMPED
C. Black	5	0	0

NOTABLE BATTING PERFORMANCES

PLAYER	OPPOSITION	SCORE
P. Ross	Dollar	58
D. Meikle	Lathallan	30*
R. Watson	Lathallan	27*
F. Cox	Cargilfield	27

NOTABLE BOWLING PERFORMANCES

PLAYER	OPPOSITION	FIGURES
P. Ross	Cargilfield	4-9
R. Clark	Riley	3-2
F. Cox	Cargilfield	3-7
N. Farrar	Riley	3-9
M. Brown	Loretto	3-16

CRANLEIGH

Horseshoe Lane, Cranleigh, Surrey GU6 8QH
Tel: 01483 542051 Fax: 01483 277136
Email: rcg@cranprep.org
Headmaster: M. Roulston Master i/c Cricket: Robin Gainher

2005 SEASON

Played: 10   Won: 5   Lost: 2   Drawn: 3

Captain: J. Kinsey

Team selected from: J. Kinsey*, A. Goudie*, P. Lyle, T. Forster,
A. Powell, M. Mockford, T. Campbell, H. Jolly, C. Rollings,
G. Cross, M. Date-Chong, J. Hughes, M. Haynes,
T. Batchelor, C. Kimmins.

SUMMARY

With a record of five wins and two 'winning draws', the 2005
1st XI can look back on their season with a great deal of
satisfaction. With the preferred option of batting first, the team
enjoyed the challenge of setting a target and then bowling the
opposition out. Wins came against Ashdown House, Highfield,
Edgeborough, Hurstpierpoint and Parkside. The draws were
against Cottesmore, Milbourne Lodge and Papplewick and the
disappointing losses to Westbourne House and Eagle House.

James Kinsey led from the front, scoring nearly 300 runs
and taking 17 wickets. Other major contributors with the bat
were Tom Forster, Peers Lyle, Josh Hughes and Charlie
Kimmins (a colt who played three 1st XI matches).

Bowling honours went to Tom Campbell and Gus Powell,
who both return in 2006, and to the 'spin twins' Andrew Goudie
and Michael 'Shane' Haynes. Hugh Jolly, Charlie Rollings, Tom
Batchelor and Michael Mockford all contributed with either bat
or ball and return next year. Of this year's squad, eight players
return in 2006, promising another potentially exciting year for
Cranleigh.

AVERAGES

BATSMAN	INNINGS	NOT OUT	RUNS	H. SCORE	AVERAGE
T. Batchelor	4	3	40	22*	40.0
C. Kimmins	3	0	97	39	32.3
J. Kinsey	10	1	285	70*	31.7
T. Forster	10	1	160	76*	17.8
J. Hughes	10	4	96	33*	16.0
P. Lyle	8	1	71	27	10.1

BOWLER	OVERS	MAIDENS	RUNS	WICKETS	AVERAGE
C. Kimmins	11	0	51	7	7.3
J. Kinsey	61	20	163	17	9.6
T. Campbell	48	6	205	17	12.1
A. Goudie	53	4	244	16	15.2
A. Powell	38	7	115	7	16.4
M. Haynes	39	6	173	8	21.6

WICKET-KEEPER	PLAYED	CAUGHT	STUMPED
J. Hughes	10	4	4

NOTABLE BATTING PERFORMANCES

PLAYER	OPPOSITION	SCORE
T. Forster	Highfield	76*
J. Kinsey	Milbourne Lodge	70*
J. Kinsey	Edgeborough	70
J. Kinsey	Parkside	67

NOTABLE BOWLING PERFORMANCES

PLAYER	OPPOSITION	FIGURES
T. Campbell	Milbourne Lodge	4-3
A. Goudie	Ashdown House	4-23
M. Haynes	Edgeborough	4-26
A. Goudie	Eagle House	4-39

DORSET HOUSE

The Manor, Bury, Pulborough, West Sussex RH20 1PB

Tel: 01798 831456 Fax: 01798 831141

Email: headmaster@dorsethouse.w-sussex.sch.uk

Headmaster: E.C. Clark   Master i/c Cricket: T. Dawes

2005 SEASON

Played: 9   Won: 5   Lost: 3   Drawn: 1

Captain: M. Donegan

Team selected from: M. Donegan*, W. Harrison*, T. Chase*,
H. Godman-Dorington*, J. Edgcumbe-Rendle, J. Ware,
H. Bentley*, S. Chase, J. Wolfe, J. Ellis*, W. Truscott,
D. Podlasinski*, O. Gale, M. Jermyn.

Scorer: A. Drummond

SUMMARY

Both pupils and staff alike will remember the 2005 season for Dorset House with great affection. More boys than ever played cricket for the school, and, unlike 2004, the weather did not play a major part in disrupting games. We had an extraordinary number of thrilling finishes at all levels and every team played a mixture of both limited over and declaration cricket.

The 1st XI had a successful season, winning the majority of their matches. Only against Woodcote House did the boys let themselves down. Thankfully, true to the spirit of the school, they fought back in their next two games and won both.

The team were well led by Matthew Donegan, while Josh Ware looked a quality player for next season. They played attacking cricket and, most importantly of all, played the game wholeheartedly and with enthusiasm. This was reflected in the boys' fielding which was at times outstanding.

BATSMAN	INNINGS	NOT OUT	RUNS	H. SCORE	AVERAGE
M. Donegan	9	0	222	59	24.7
J. Ware	9	1	156	52	19.5
H. Godman-Dorington	9	2	122	41	17.4
W. Harrison	8	0	118	39	14.8
M. Jermyn	2	1	12	7	12.0
T. Chase	9	2	77	17	11.0

BOWLER	OVERS	MAIDENS	RUNS	WICKETS	AVERAGE
M. Donegan	51	-	173	19	9.1
H. Godman-Dorington	34	-	157	13	12.1
T. Chase	30	-	117	7	16.7
J. Ware	17.2	-	96	5	19.2
J. Edgcumbe-Rendle	12	-	77	3	25.7

NOTABLE BATTING PERFORMANCES

PLAYER	OPPOSITION	
M. Donegan	Duke of Kent	59
M. Donegan	Windlesham	52
J. Ware	Windlesham	52

Did you know? . . . Graham Gooch holds the record for the most number of runs in Tests for England. He scored 2632 runs in Ashes Tests but started his Test career with a duck in each innings against Australia at Edgbaston.

DULWICH COLLEGE

42 Alleyn Park, London SE21 7AA

Tel: 020 8670 3217 Fax: 020 8766 7586

Email: registrar@dcpslondon.org

Headmaster: G. Marsh   Master i/c Cricket: Robin Whitcomb

2005 SEASON

Played: 11   Won: 5   Lost: 4   Drawn: 2

Captain: T. Deasy   Vice-captain: W. MacVicar

Team selected from: T. Deasy*, W. MacVicar*, J. Joyce*, H. Browne*, P. Patel*, S. Holland*, R. Ingleby-MacKenzie*, C. Prentice*, B. Barron*, E. Phillips, E. Davies, W. Clay, A. McCalla, E. Oram.

Scorer: T. Renner

SUMMARY

This was another very enjoyable and successful season. The highlight was to win through to the JET competition finals at St. Edward's Oxford, where we lost narrowly to Millfield.

There were some outstanding cricketers in the team. The captain Tom Deasy played for Surrey, as did William MacVicar and Harry Browne. Deasy's 149* against a touring South African side was superb. MacVicar and Browne were two good all-rounders and there was excellent spin bowling from Purav Patel and Sam Holland, who took 40 wickets between them. Jasper Joyce was a most impressive keeper.

The future looks very promising with some talented cricketers coming through.

AVERAGES

BATSMAN	INNINGS	NOT OUT	RUNS	H. SCORE	AVERAGE
T. Deasy	12	2	387	149*	38.7
W. MacVicar	12	4	308	69*	38.5
H. Browne	11	2	128	31*	14.2

BOWLER	OVERS	MAIDENS	RUNS	WICKETS	AVERAGE
S. Holland	52	4	201	23	8.7
P. Patel	51	4	193	17	11.4
W. MacVicar	55	9	209	11	19.0
H. Browne	48	8	194	7	27.7

WICKET-KEEPER	PLAYED	CAUGHT	STUMPED
J. Joyce	11	5	7

NOTABLE BATTING PERFORMANCES

PLAYER	OPPOSITION	SCORE
T. Deasy	Waterkloof (South Africa)	149*
W. MacVicar	Aldro	69*
W. MacVicar	Wellesley House	54
T. Deasy	Millfield	52

NOTABLE BOWLING PERFORMANCES

PLAYER	OPPOSITION	FIGURES
S. Holland	Wellesley House	5-23
P. Patel	Aldro	4-6
S. Holland	Aldro	4-15
S. Holland	Dulwich College	4-20

DUNHURST

Steep, Petersfield, Hampshire GU32 2DP

Tel: 01730 300200 Fax: 01730 300600

Email: dunhurst@bedales.org.uk

Headmistress: Penny Fryer   Master i/c Cricket: Mark Collins

2005 SEASON

Played: 9   Won: 5   Lost: 3   Drawn: 1

Captain: W. Rhys   Vice-captain: P. Mabe

Team selected from: W. Rhys, P. Mabe, O. Benge, O. Brand,
J. Norman, H. Russell, M. Collins-Wolff, J. Welch,
Z. Farley-Drake, G. Parker, A. Thorp, C. Wetherill,
A. Athill, K. Banks.

SUMMARY

The 2005 season was a mixed one. It started with a win in our
own Dunhurst six-a-side tournament, followed by a good win
over Great Ballard. The next week, however, we were well
beaten by local rivals Highfield. This seemed to spur the efforts
of the boys in training and the results came on the field.
Commanding wins over Boundary Oak and More House led
into an amazing fielding performance to beat St. Edmund's.

Fielding was the team's strong point, but huge improvements
were made in batting and bowling. Will Rhys opened the
batting extremely well and he was tremendously supported by
Peter Mabe. Jack Norman bowled a good line all season and
Ollie Benge and Hamish Russell proved to be excellent all-
rounders.

All in all, Dunhurst had a good season which hopefully will
lead to even better ones in the future.

AVERAGES

BATSMAN	INNINGS	NOT OUT	RUNS	H. SCORE	AVERAGE
W. Rhys	8	2	337	95*	56.2
P. Mabe	9	2	195	51*	27.9
J. Norman	7	0	81	31	11.6
H. Russell	7	2	56	20*	11.2
O. Benge	9	0	89	19	9.9
O. Brand	7	2	36	15	7.2

BOWLER	OVERS	MAIDENS	RUNS	WICKETS	AVERAGE
J. Norman	36	9	99	9	11.0
P. Mabe	37	4	140	12	11.7
O. Benge	34	1	145	11	13.2
A. Athill	10	0	47	3	15.7
H. Russell	21	0	117	3	39.0

WICKET-KEEPER	PLAYED	CAUGHT	STUMPED
W. Rhys	8	3	4

NOTABLE BATTING PERFORMANCES

PLAYER	OPPOSITION	SCORE
W. Rhys	Forres Sandle Manor	95*
W. Rhys	Boundary Oak	69
P. Mabe	Mayville HS	51*
J. Norman	Great Ballard	31

NOTABLE BOWLING PERFORMANCES

PLAYER	OPPOSITION	FIGURES
J. Norman	More House	3-2
P. Mabe	Mayville HS	3-5
O. Benge	More House	4-17
H. Russell	St. Edmund's	2-9

EAGLE HOUSE

Sandhurst, Berkshire GU47 8PH

Tel: 01344 772134 Fax: 01344 779039

Email: info@eaglehouseschool.com

Headmaster: S.J. Carder Master i/c Cricket: P.W. Whalley

2005 SEASON

Played: 9   Won: 9

Captain: O. Barker

Team selected from: O. Barker*, A. Boobbyer*, B. Mosses*,
S. Hanley*, J. Russell, P. Davidge*, K. Ross, A. Abdi,
G. Hamilton-Fairley, G. Winkler, J. Disney-May*, J. Burgin,
J. Tuckwell, F. Evans.

Scorer: S. Grange

SUMMARY

The Eagle House 1st XI of 2005 must rank as one of the finest
ever in the long cricketing history of the school. All the regular
school fixtures ended in comprehensive wins with the narrowest
margin of victory being by 5 wickets. Three further wins were
recorded in the County Twenty20 competition, the only blemish
on an outstanding record being a narrow defeat in the semi-
final. (These statistics are included in the averages).

This success was based on the dominant batting of Oliver
Barker, Angus Boobbyer and Ben Mosses who scored over 1000
runs between them. In particular, Ben Mosses destroyed
opposition attacks with powerful batting of Andrew Flintoff
proportions. The ability by this top three to score quickly was
backed up by a strong attack of seam bowlers and the leg-spin
of captain Oliver Barker. Their accuracy and penetration meant
that no side scored more than 130 against us, and on five
occasions the opposition was dismissed for less than 60. This
tight bowling was backed up by a strong commitment in the
field. All in all it was an exceptional season, enjoyed by a fine
bunch of hard-working cricketers.

AVERAGES

BATSMAN	INNINGS	NOT OUT	RUNS	H. SCORE	AVERAGE
B. Mosses	11	6	483	89*	96.6
A. Boobbyer	11	5	369	69	61.5
O. Barker	11	1	235	51	23.5
G. Hamilton-Fairley	3	2	18	9*	18.0
S. Hanley	8	3	82	19*	16.4
P. Davidge	4	3	16	14*	16.0

BOWLER	OVERS	MAIDENS	RUNS	WICKETS	AVERAGE
A. Boobbyer	64	13	145	26	5.6
P. Davidge	62	11	157	22	7.1
J. Disney-May	45	7	154	18	8.6
K. Ross	24	5	105	9	11.7
O. Barker	43	4	183	15	12.2
S. Hanley	32	3	128	5	25.6

WICKET-KEEPER	PLAYED	CAUGHT	STUMPED
B. Mosses	10	7	9
F. Evans	1	1	0

NOTABLE BATTING PERFORMANCES

PLAYER	OPPOSITION	SCORE
B. Mosses	Parkside	89*
B. Mosses	Bearwood	79*
A. Boobbyer	Forest	69
B. Mosses	Charters	67
B. Mosses	Crawford (South Africa)	62*
A. Boobbyer	Cranleigh	54
O. Barker	Bearwood	51

NOTABLE BOWLING PERFORMANCES

PLAYER	OPPOSITION	FIGURES
P. Davidge	Cranleigh	7-3-9-5
A. Boobbyer	Crawford (South Africa)	5-0-23-5
O. Barker	Charters	3-1-5-4
A. Boobbyer	Highfield	5-1-5-4
O. Barker	Bearwood	3-0-7-4
P. Davidge	Ludgrove	8-3-9-4
A. Boobbyer	Crosfields	6-0-11-3

EDGEGROVE

Aldenham Village, Herts WD25 8NL

Tel: 01923 855724 Fax: 01923 859920

Email: enquiries@edgegrove.indschools.co.uk

Headmaster: M.T. Wilson Master i/c Cricket: L. Holder

2005 SEASON

Played: 7 Won: 3 Drawn: 4

Captains : S. Wilson and H. Sinclair

Team selected from: H. Sinclair*, M. Stear*, S. Wilson*,
A. Comfort, H. Khawaja, R. Handelaar, J. Cartwright,
J. Johnson-Crooks, S. Brown, I. Hara, E. Forson, C. Leigh.

SUMMARY

The cricket season of 2005 was an excellent one for the boys. They enjoyed all their matches and played some inspirational cricket. The team was amiably led by S. Wilson and H. Sinclair who both made valuable contributions with bat and ball.

Notable performances were M. Stear's impressive 84 against Swanbourne House and S. Wilson's 5-10 against Beechwood Park. The highlight of the season was our tussle against Heath Mount, which ended in a very tight finish, with each of the players contributing to the final total. I would like to commend all the boys on their effort and commitment to the team, both on and off the field.

Did you know? . . . The highest individual score for England in Tests remains the 364 scored by Len Hutton against Australia at The Oval in 1938.

AVERAGES

BATSMAN	INNINGS	NOT OUT	RUNS	H. SCORE	AVERAGE
M. Stear	7	2	218	84	43.6
S. Wilson	7	3	136	43	34.0
H. Sinclair	7	1	176	64	29.3
A. Comfort	5	1	85	30	21.2

BOWLER	OVERS	MAIDENS	RUNS	WICKETS	AVERAGE
H. Sinclair	39	11	39	7	5.6
S. Wilson	36	7	84	13	6.5
A. Comfort	16.3	0	82	6	13.7
R. Handelaar	28	2	95	6	15.8
W. Khawaja	24	3	95	6	15.8

WICKET-KEEPER	PLAYED	CAUGHT	STUMPED
M. Stear	7	0	3

NOTABLE BATTING PERFORMANCES

PLAYER	OPPOSITION	SCORE
M. Stear	Swanbourne House	84
H. Sinclair	Heath Mount	64
M. Stear	Beechwood Park	57
H. Sinclair	Beechwood Park	62
S. Wilson	Beechwood Park	43

NOTABLE BOWLING PERFORMANCES

PLAYER	OPPOSITION	FIGURES
S. Wilson	Beechwood Park	7-1-10-5
H. Sinclair	Lockers Park	7-4-8-4

THE ELMS

Colwall, Malvern, Worcestershire WR13 6EF

Tel: 01684 540344 Fax: 01684 541174

Email: office@elmsschool.co.uk

Headmaster: L.A.C. Ashby   Master i/c Cricket: Grenville Simons

2005 SEASON

Played: 7   Won: 3   Lost: 1   Drawn: 3

Captain: J. Croft

Team selected from: J. Croft*, H. Amor, G. Lacey, T. Claydon, R. Oxley, S. Siviter, A. Ross, G. Hazell, J. Paterson, G. Lee, J. Mainwaring, W. McAleer.

Scorers: Cora Marr and David Lu

SUMMARY

The term began with a flurry of runs. Openers James Croft and George Lacey put on 115 in the first match and followed this up with a school record partnership of 211.

James Croft led the side with purpose. He kept wicket very tidily and when at the crease displayed a wide range of attractive scoring shots. George Lacey proved to be a reliable opening partner while Henry Amor, Alexander Ross, Sam Siviter and Tom Claydon chipped in with some useful scores.

Henry and Alex led the bowling attack, supported by Tom and Sam. While they took wickets, their direction was all too often rather wayward. James Mainwaring and George Lacey provided the alternative spin option, their flight and turn causing batsmen some problems.

Apart from a heavy defeat at the hands of Beaudesert Park, the boys enjoyed a reasonably successful season which was recorded in the scorebook by David Lu and our first girl scorer, Cora Marr.

AVERAGES

BATSMAN	INNINGS	NOT OUT	RUNS	H. SCORE	AVERAGE
J. Croft	7	1	347	117*	57.8
G. Lacey	7	1	125	71*	20.8
T. Claydon	5	2	42	21*	14.0
H. Amor	6	1	59	19*	11.8
A. Ross	6	1	53	27	10.6
S. Siviter	4	1	21	18*	7.0

BOWLER	OVERS	MAIDENS	RUNS	WICKETS	AVERAGE
J. Mainwaring	14	4	31	7	4.4
H. Amor	39	8	108	16	6.7
A. Ross	37	10	97	9	10.8
G. Lacey	13	1	45	3	15.0
S. Siviter	11	4	30	2	15.0
T. Claydon	27	9	69	3	23.0

WICKET-KEEPER	PLAYED	CAUGHT	STUMPED
J. Croft	7	3	4

NOTABLE BATTING PERFORMANCES

PLAYER	OPPOSITION	SCORE
J. Croft	Tockington Manor	70
J. Croft	The Downs	117*
G. Lacey	The Downs	71*
J. Croft	Hillstone	60

NOTABLE BOWLING PERFORMANCES

PLAYER	OPPOSITION	FIGURES
H. Amor	Tockington Manor	8-4-8-5
J. Mainwaring	The Downs	6-2-10-4

FOREMARKE HALL

Milton, Derbyshire DE65 6EJ

Tel: 01283 703269 Fax: 01283 701185

Email: office@foremarke.org.uk

Headmaster: P. H. Brewster   Master i/c Cricket: J. Debenham

2005 SEASON

Played: 15   Won: 12   Lost: 1   Drawn: 2

Captain: M. Jacques   Vice-captain: T. Cosford

Team selected from: M. Jacques*, T. Cosford*, O. Dancey*, L. Duggan*, H. Rees-Jones*, D. Wood*, J. Challener, A. Clarke-Dowson, M. Hodges, R. Keep, B. Larimore, C. Twigg, J. Bird, J. Golding, J. Lewis.

Scorer: Mrs E. Wood

SUMMARY

This was an outstanding season for the 1st XI with an impressive twelve victories from fifteen games. The side was intelligently led by Michael Jacques, who combined a large volume of runs at the top of the order with some increasingly astute captaincy in the field. The top order were consistently impressive with Michael, Oliver Dancey, Tom Cosford and Huw Rees-Jones contributing twelve half centuries and over 1300 runs between them.

With this sort of platform the bowlers were able to bowl with attacking fields and Tom Cosford, Luke Duggan and Daniel Wood took full advantage, all taking over 20 wickets each. Tight fielding and catching helped to keep pressure on opposing batsmen. There were particularly impressive victories against Bedford, King's Canterbury, Trent and S. Anselm's. The only defeat was a disappointing performance in the JET quarter-final against a strong Malsis XI. With such a strong Year 8 the opportunities for Year 7 were limited. Andrew Clarke-Dowson and Matthew Hodges improved their bowling as the term progressed. They will both be important members of a rather inexperienced side next year.

AVERAGES

BATSMAN	INNINGS	NOT OUT	RUNS	H. SCORE	AVERAGE
M. Jacques	15	7	474	73*	59.3
T. Cosford	14	6	353	77	44.1
O. Dancey	14	6	289	65	36.1
H. Rees-Jones	11	4	207	76*	29.6
J. Challener	11	3	139	39	17.4

BOWLER	OVERS	MAIDENS	RUNS	WICKETS	AVERAGE
L. Duggan	63.3	11	150	22	6.8
T. Cosford	63.4	13	192	23	8.3
C. Twigg	29.3	5	114	10	11.4
D. Wood	61.3	1	259	21	12.3
M. Hodges	59.4	9	199	13	15.3
M. Clarke-Dowson	44	5	188	10	18.8

WICKET-KEEPER	PLAYED	CAUGHT	STUMPED
H. Rees-Jones	15	9	2

NOTABLE BATTING PERFORMANCES

PLAYER	OPPOSITION	SCORE
T. Cosford	Ranby House	77
H. Rees-Jones	Princethorpe	76*
M. Jacques	Derby Grammar	73*
T. Cosford	Bilton Grange	68*
M. Jacques	Birchfield	66*
O. Dancey	Birchfield	65
T. Cosford	Malsis	64*

NOTABLE BOWLING PERFORMANCES

PLAYER	OPPOSITION	FIGURES
D. Wood	S. Anselm's	5-29
D. Wood	Repton U14	4-6
T. Cosford	Bedford Modern	4-28
A. Clarke-Dowson	Mount St. Mary's	3-3
C. Twigg	Mount St. Mary's	3-3
L. Duggan	Maidwell Hall	3-4
L. Duggan	King's Canterbury	3-7

HALL GROVE

London Road, Bagshot, Surrey GU19 5HZ
Tel: 01276 473059 Fax: 01276 452003
Email: registrar@hallgrove.surrey.sch.uk
Headmaster: A.R. Graham   Master i/c Cricket: T.J.G. Lewis

2005 SEASON

Played: 12   Won: 3   Lost: 6   Drawn: 3

Captain: A. Parkes   Vice-captain: R. Houghton-Berry

Team selected from: A. Parkes*, R. Houghton-Berry*, R. Jones,
S. Boatman, S. Carver, R. Chisholm, A. Colville, J. Gaffney,
E. Graham, T. Hughes, W. Hughes, A. O' Meara, A. Richardson.

Scorer: S. Sharpe

SUMMARY

A mixed season for a young side, with three brilliant victories
against Shrewsbury House, Ludgrove and Woodcote House,
coupled with defeats at the hands of Parkside, Homefield, Hoe
Bridge, Aldro, Papplewick and St. John's Beaumont. There
were also three draws against Sunningdale, St. Andrew's and
Bishopsgate. Many of the defeats were close encounters where
perhaps a little more belief might have won the day. The team
comprised mainly Year 7 boys so this represents a fair return
and there is great potential for next year.

Alasdair Parkes led the side with great skill and good
tactical awareness. He scored over 200 runs and formed the
backbone of the batting, although there were good contributions
from the youngsters, Colville, Chisholm and Gaffney. Ryan
Houghton-Berry led the bowling attack taking 13 wickets,
bowling particularly well as the season progressed. There was
strong support from Jones, Boatman and Chisholm. The side's
fielding was generally good, with the majority of catches being
held, and the ground fielding was solid. Alasdair Parkes proved
to be an able keeper. An enjoyable season.

AVERAGES

BATSMAN	INNINGS	NOT OUT	RUNS	H. SCORE	AVERAGE
A. Parkes	12	3	219	56	24.3
A. Colville	9	1	134	36	16.8
J. Gaffney	11	2	88	17	9.8
R. Chisholm	12	1	95	24	8.6
R. Houghton-Berry	9	2	50	20	7.1
A. O'Meara	11	0	73	21	6.6

BOWLER	OVERS	MAIDENS	RUNS	WICKETS	AVERAGE
R. Houghton-Berry	47	4	158	13	12.2
S. Boatman	28.4	3	99	8	12.4
R. Chisholm	35	3	155	12	12.9
S. Carver	10	0	55	3	18.3
R. Jones	49.2	6	206	10	20.6
A. Colville	40.5	3	148	3	49.3

WICKET-KEEPER	PLAYED	CAUGHT	STUMPED
A. Parkes	12	8	0

NOTABLE BATTING PERFORMANCES

PLAYER	OPPOSITION	SCORE
A. Parkes	Sunningdale	56
A. Parkes	St. Andrew's	45
A. Colville	Aldro	36
A. Parkes	Hoe Bridge	29
A. Colville	St. John's	25
R. Chisholm	Parkside	24
A. O'Meara	Shrewsbury House	21

NOTABLE BOWLING PERFORMANCES

PLAYER	OPPOSITION	FIGURES
R. Houghton-Berry	Woodcote House	4-7
R. Chisholm	Ludgrove	4-10
S. Boatman	Shrewsbury House	3-8
R. Jones	Sunningdale	3-22
S. Carver	Shrewsbury House	2-6

HANDCROSS PARK

Handcross, Haywards Heath, West Sussex RH17 6HF

Tel: 01444 400526 Fax: 01444 400527

Email: iclark@handxpark.com

Headmaster: W. Hilton Master i/c Cricket: Iain Clark

2005 SEASON

Played: 9   Won: 7   Drawn: 2

Captain: J. Johnson   Vice-captain: T. Johnson

Team selected from: L. Berney, R. Bush, J. Johnson*,
J. Rivers*, H. Wake, C. White, T. Hodgson, T. Johnson*,
N. O'Dwyer, T. Rivers, F. Ziyada.

SUMMARY

In a complete turn around from the 2004 season, where the boys only managed two victories, this season the 1st XI were undefeated, a fantastic achievement. The team was spearheaded by James Johnson, the captain, ably assisted by brother Tom and the Rivers brothers, Joseph and Theo, who set our top order alive. Further down the order there was plenty of depth and support, all boys playing their part to help ensure that our unbeaten season remained intact.

The biggest accolade I can pay the boys is that their team spirit and collective desire was evident, not just to play well, but to win matches.

A big thank you to Malcolm Carter, the 1st XI coach, who set high standards for the boys and always looked out for their interests in the true spirit of the game.

AVERAGES

BATSMAN	INNINGS	NOT OUT	RUNS	H. SCORE	AVERAGE
J. Johnson	9	2	272	62	38.9
T. Johnson	9	3	222	65	37.0
J. Rivers	8	2	115	45*	19.2
T. Rivers	7	3	72	42*	18.0
C. White	6	3	31	11	10.3
L. Berney	6	1	46	19	9.2

BOWLER	OVERS	MAIDENS	RUNS	WICKETS	AVERAGE
C. White	26	4	79	11	7.2
T. Rivers	33	4	115	12	9.6
J. Johnson	46	6	140	12	11.7
T. Johnson	50.1	3	167	14	11.9
J. Rivers	38	7	95	6	15.8
L. Berney	19	1	70	3	23.3

NOTABLE BATTING PERFORMANCES

PLAYER	OPPOSITION	H. SCOREE
J. Johnson	St. Aubyn's	62
J. Johnson	Brambletye	50
J. Johnson	Pennthorpe	58*
T. Johnson	Brambletye	46*
T. Johnson	Cumnor House	65
J. Rivers	Cumnor House	45*
J. Rivers	Cumnor House	42*

NOTABLE BOWLING PERFORMANCES

PLAYER	OPPOSITION	FIGURES
J. Johnson	St. Aubyn's	3-20
J. Johnson	Pennthorpe	4-18
T. Johnson	Brambletye	3-14
T. Johnson	Ardingly	4-14
T. Rivers	Brambletye	5-4
T. Rivers	Duke of Kent	3-10
C. White	Cumnor House	4-5

THE HAWTHORNS

Pendell Court, Bletchingly, Surrey RH1 4QJ

Tel: 01883 742798 Fax: 01883 744256

Email: office@hawthorns.com

Headmaster: T. Johns   Master i/c Cricket: A. Duggan

2005 SEASON

Played: 9   Won: 2   Lost: 6   Drawn: 1

Captain: C. Hawes

Team selected from: C. Hawes*, A. Ewen*, F. Watts*, J. Bleach*, H. Waddilove*, O. Wilkinson*, J. Fortune*, D. Hamilton*, C. Hickey*, W. Bouch, H. Tye, T. Ganley.

SUMMARY

The Hawthorns' batting was opened by F. Watts, who showed tenacity and natural ability. The pick of the batsmen, however, was H. Tye, who played several important innings at an average of 32. The captain, C. Hawes, encouraged well in the field but with the bat, a more steadying influence was often required. J. Bleach, A. Ewen, C. Hickey and O. Wilkinson proved that they too could strike out, but their position in the order often meant they were required to hit runs quickly.

Opening the bowling is never easy, but H. Waddilove and T. Ganley appeared to relish their role. Time and again their combined eight overs would place pressure upon the opponents. O. Wilkinson, J. Fortune and D. Hamilton could always be relied upon to get wickets at vital times.

Unfortunately there remained a flaw in the character of the team. Rather than build upon the momentum generated from a wicket, a tight spell of bowling or an effective batting partnership, the advantage was rarely exploited and frequently handed back. There were too few victories and at least three defeats could have been avoided.

AVERAGES

BATSMAN	INNINGS	NOT OUT	RUNS	H. SCORE	AVERAGE
H. Tye	11	2	290	57*	32.2
F. Watts	9	1	136	39*	17.0
O. Wilkinson	6	1	62	27	12.4
C. Hawes	8	1	75	23	10.7

BOWLER	OVERS	MAIDENS	RUNS	WICKETS	AVERAGE
H. Waddilove	32	2	101	15	6.7
J. Fortune	16	2	99	8	12.4
O. Wilkinson	23	0	108	8	13.5
C. Hawes	16	1	82	5	16.4

WICKET-KEEPER	PLAYED	CAUGHT	STUMPED
J. Bleach	9	2	2

NOTABLE BATTING PERFORMANCES

PLAYER	OPPOSITION	SCORE
H. Tye	Yardley Court	57*
F. Watts	Kingswood House	39*

NOTABLE BOWLING PERFORMANCES

PLAYER	OPPOSITION	FIGURES
O. Wilkinson	Priory	3-6
H. Waddilove	St. Michael's	3-7
H. Waddilove	Kingswood House	4-12
J. Fortune	Cumnor House	4-9
J. Fortune	Yardley Court	3-22
H. Waddilove	Old Hawthornian	4-14

HAZLEGROVE

Sparkford, Nr. Yeovil, Somerset BA22 7JA

Tel: 01963 440314 Fax: 01963 440569

Email: office@hazlegrove.somerset.sch.uk

Headmaster: R. Fenwick Master i/c Cricket: A.D.J. Baker

2005 SEASON

Played: 12   Won: 3   Lost: 2   Drawn: 7

Captain: G. Mann   Vice-captain: J. Saunders

Team selected from: G. Mann*, J. Saunders*, T. Gibbs,
T. Down, O. Farrer, N. Charlier, J. Burke, E. Johnson,
J. Montgomery, F. McKechnie, J. Wilson-Brown,
T. Hunt, A. Horsington.

Scorers: P. Higgs and J. Perry

SUMMARY

Although this was not a vintage season, it was a very enjoyable term's cricket. It soon became apparent that we did not possess an out-and-out match-winner or star batsman or bowler. We did, however, possess an excellent team spirit and an intelligent captain who was able to make the most of the resources on offer.

George Mann led from the front, scoring over 200 runs and taking the most wickets. He captained the side very well and displayed a promising 'cricket brain'. He was ably supported by Josh Saunders, who ended the season as a reliable opening batsman and tidy keeper. Oli Farrer, Tom Down and Nick Charlier all made important contributions with both bat and ball, whilst John Montgomery proved to be a promising left-arm seamer. No one bowler was able to bowl consistently well and as a result we were rarely able to force a win.

Despite this, the 2005 1st XI were a pleasure to coach as they worked together as a team so well, and were keen and enthusiastic about the game. Several boys go on to their senior schools as promising cricketers and a talented core remain to carry on the mantle.

AVERAGES

BATSMAN	INNINGS	NOT OUT	RUNS	H. SCORE	AVERAGE
N. Charlier	4	3	31	17*	31.0
G. Mann	11	2	203	50*	22.6
J. Saunders	11	3	143	47*	17.9
T. Gibbs	10	2	125	26	15.6
T. Down	11	0	141	30	12.8

BOWLER	OVERS	MAIDENS	RUNS	WICKETS	AVERAGE
O. Farrer	41	6	143	9	15.9
G. Mann	37	3	196	11	17.8
J. Montgomery	50	9	181	10	18.1
N. Charlier	30	2	129	6	21.5
T. Down	44	2	204	7	29.1

WICKET-KEEPER	PLAYED	CAUGHT	STUMPED
J. Saunders	12	8	3

NOTABLE BATTING PERFORMANCES

PLAYER	OPPOSITION	SCORE
G. Mann	Fathers	50*
J. Saunders	Millfield	47*
G. Mann	Monkton Combe	44*
G. Mann	Taunton	43
G. Mann	Dolphin	33
J. Saunders	Clayesmore	31
T. Down	Crawford	30

NOTABLE BOWLING PERFORMANCES

PLAYER	OPPOSITION	FIGURES
J. Montgomery	Dolphin	5-1-12-4
G. Mann	Fathers	3-0-12-3
G. Mann	Dolphin	3-0-16-3
J. Montgomery	King's Hall	7-1-27-3

HOE BRIDGE

Hoe Place, Old Woking Road, Woking, Surrey GU22 8JE
Tel: 01483 757262 Fax: 01483 757262
Email: sport@hoebridgeschool.co.uk
Headmaster: R. Barr   Master i/c Cricket: Graham Scott

2005 SEASON

Played: 7   Won: 3   Lost: 2   Drawn: 2

Captain: T. Wood   Vice-captain: D. Hunt

Team selected from: T. Wood, D. Hunt, A. Milton, J. Lambroza,
A. Coles, W. Oliver, J. Dickson, H. Adolphus, F. Imrie,
A. Knox, E. Strang, D. Wardle, J. Williams.

Scorer: M. Wane

SUMMARY

The season began in March with a tour to St. Lucia. We played six matches, all against U15 sides, and we managed to win one game, the highlight of the tour being our match played at the Beausejour Test ground. The tour prepared us well for the season, although the early season rain disrupted our first few matches.

At times the team performed to a high standard and were complimented by the opposition, but they had their off-days as well.

Tommy Wood was outstanding with the bat, and when he performed so did the team. Seven of the side are available next year and we were disappointed not to progress past the semi-final in the Surrey Prep Schools' Cup.

> *Did you know?* . . . The fastest century for England in Tests is the 75 minutes (76 balls) it took for Gilbert Jessop against the Australians at the Oval in 1902.

AVERAGES

BATSMAN	INNINGS	NOT OUT	RUNS	H. SCORE	AVERAGE
T. Wood	7	3	289	102*	72.3
A. Milton	4	3	26	14*	26.0
D. Hunt	7	2	102	60*	20.4
H. Adolphus	6	0	113	53	18.8
J. Williams	6	0	79	23	13.2

BOWLER	OVERS	MAIDENS	RUNS	WICKETS	AVERAGE
E. Strang	26.2	2	77	15	5.1
J. Lambroza	31	2	117	8	14.6
T. Wood	28	3	124	8	15.5
A. Milton	22	4	103	6	17.2
D. Hunt	28	3	133	7	19.0

WICKET-KEEPER	PLAYED	CAUGHT	STUMPED
H. Adolphus	6	6	0
D. Wardle	1	2	0

NOTABLE BATTING PERFORMANCES

PLAYER	OPPOSITION	SCORE
T. Wood	Hall Grove	102*
T. Wood	Parkside	61*
T. Wood	KCS Wimbledon	51*
D. Hunt	Hall Grove	60*
H. Adolphus	Chinthurst	53

NOTABLE BOWLING PERFORMANCES

PLAYER	OPPOSITION	FIGURES
E. Strang	Cranmore	7-12
A. Milton	KCS Wimbledon	3-23

HOLME GRANGE

Heathlands Road, Wokingham, Berkshire RG40 3AL

Tel: 0118 978 1566 Fax: 0118 977 0810

Email: school@holmegrange.org

Headmaster: N.J. Brodrick Master i/c Cricket: P.V. Miles

2005 SEASON

Played: 6   Won: 3   Lost: 3

Captain: O. Miles   Vice-captain: I. Sears

Team selected from: O. Clarke, E. Cole, K. de' Ath, O. Miles*,
I. Sears*, H. Cartwright, R. Grier, R. MacSwan, J. Mann,
J. O'Connor, J. Powell, O. Powell.

SUMMARY

With two county standard players in the team, the season started with great expectations but, rather like the weather, the results were a little disappointing. Our three victories were recorded against St. Andrew's, St. Neot's and Lambrook Haileybury.

The most enthralling match was a 25 over game played on a baking hot summer's day against Bearwood. Bearwood batted first and Matthew Bell (Berkshire) hit an impressive 91 with Bearwood closing on 147-8. Oliver Miles (another Berkshire player) almost equalled Matthew's effort. Oliver scored 82 and was out early in the final over. Holme Grange narrowly missed victory, closing on 140-3. Ian Sears bowled well in this match with his pinpoint accurate in-swinging yorkers. Ian took 4 wickets for 15 runs off his allotted 5 overs.

This year will be remembered mainly because of the efforts of Oliver Miles and Ian Sears. Oliver opened in every match; he batted through in three matches and averaged 84.3. Ian Sears bowled with real pace and accuracy and took 15 wickets at an average of 5.2. These two players will be greatly missed next season.

AVERAGES

BATSMAN	INNINGS	NOT OUT	RUNS	H. SCORE	AVERAGE
O. Miles	6	3	253	82	84.3
O. Clarke	6	2	74	28*	18.5

BOWLER	OVERS	MAIDENS	RUNS	WICKETS	AVERAGE
I. Sears	27.3	3	78	15	5.2
O. Clarke	34.3	2	118	11	10.7
J. Mann	15	1	60	5	12.0
O. Miles	17	2	89	6	14.8
K. de'Ath	25	3	94	5	18.8

WICKET-KEEPER	PLAYED	CAUGHT	STUMPED
O. Miles	6	4	2

NOTABLE BATTING PERFORMANCES

PLAYER	OPPOSITION	SCORE
O. Miles	Bearwood College	82
O. Miles	Ludgrove	48*

NOTABLE BOWLING PERFORMANCES

PLAYER	OPPOSITION	FIGURES
I. Sears	Bearwood College	4-15

Did you know? . . . On his Ashes debut for Australia in 1972, Bob Massie took sixteen wickets at Lord's, finishing with figures of 16-137. It became known as 'Massie's match'.

SCHOOL CRICKET GROUNDS
Hazlegrove

by Old Mower

Hazlegrove School is situated in beautiful parkland on the western edge of Blackmore Vale. Gazing across the cricket ground from the snug little scorebox, one is reminded of previous centuries - and not only those made by schoolboys, since the school was established on the site in 1947.

Evidence suggests that there has been a settlement here since the Middle Ages and it is thought that the cricket field stands on ground once covered by farm buildings and part of a small hamlet. Indeed it is not difficult to picture a rural idyll of shepherds at play beneath the splendid, old oak trees.

The square looks impressive, but that is hardly surprising for the head groundsman, John Atkins, is a cricket fanatic: three tonnes of loam are spread over the area every autumn.

Opened in 1960, the pavilion, with its wooden floor worn by generations of boys' studs, is where cricket master Andrew Baker carefully stores the 'summer game' equipment and gradually adds to the memorabilia which adorns the walls.

For a fielder on this ground, there can be no better place to while away the afternoon than on the boundary, close to the regal Cedar of Lebanon tree. Whether watching bowlers enjoy a green Somerset wicket in April and May, or batsmen making hay on the harder surfaces in June and July, the appreciative fieldsman will delight in his surroundings.

In the foreground stands the magnificent 'King John Oak', reputed to be one thousand years old, while Glastonbury Tor - the Isle of Avalon, where legend has it that King Arthur is said to be buried - rises majestically in the distance. There is more to cricket at Hazlegrove than scores, figures and results.

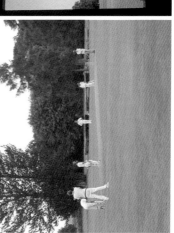

Scenes of cricket at Hazlegrove, along with the view from the scorebox and the main House

HOLMEWOOD HOUSE

Langton Green, Nr. Tunbridge Wells, Kent TN3 0EB

Tel: 01892 860000 Fax: 01892 863970

Email: admin@holmewood.kent.sch.uk

Headmaster: A. Corbett Master i/c Cricket: P. Morgan-Jones

2005 SEASON

Played: 15   Won: 9   Lost: 2   Drawn: 4

Joint Captains: T. Elliott and C. Munton

Team selected from: C. Munton*, T. Elliott*, C. Atkinson*, F. Ray, J. Chappatte, A. Norman, R. Noble, T. Liddiard, P. Trevor, T. Jenner, T. Bishop.

SUMMARY

This was a truly memorable season with positive cricket, a number of notable individual performances, a tremendous team spirit and a sense of enjoyment. The side was jointly captained by two fine cricketers in Tom Elliott and Charlie Munton. Tom scored 481 runs, including the top score of the season of 76 against Junior Kings Canterbury. His other fifties came against Newlands, Skinners, Ashdown House and DPS London.

Charlie led the attack and bowling at a fiery pace, richly deserved his haul of 22 wickets (the victims in his 5-6 against TWBG were all bowled). This bowling was well supported by Tom Jenner, Tom Liddiard, Tom Bishop, Patrick Trevor and Tom Elliott and there was great variation within this bowling attack. A tremendous innings of 67* against New Beacon by keeper/batsman Christopher Atkinson, together with a super knock of 65 by Andrew Norman against St. Bede's and 72 by Charlie Munton against Tunbridge Wells Boys Grammar, meant healthy scores could be posted. There are exciting times ahead as five boys remain next year and a tour of South Africa is planned for 2006.

AVERAGES

BATSMAN	INNINGS	NOT OUT	RUNS	H. SCORE	AVERAGE
T. Elliott	14	5	481	76	53.4
C. Atkinson	9	4	203	67*	40.6
C. Munton	12	4	212	72	26.5
F. Ray	13	2	172	36*	15.6
A. Norman	12	1	154	65	14.0
J. Chappatte	8	1	87	31	12.4

BOWLER	OVERS	MAIDENS	RUNS	WICKETS	AVERAGE
C. Munton	57.1	15	136	22	6.2
T. Bishop	41.3	10	108	14	7.7
T. Jenner	56	9	128	12	10.7
T. Elliott	46	8	149	13	11.5
T. Liddiard	44.1	5	130	9	14.4
P. Trevor	46	9	136	8	17.0

WICKET-KEEPER	PLAYED	CAUGHT	STUMPED
C. Atkinson	15	6	1

NOTABLE BATTING PERFORMANCES

PLAYER	OPPOSITION	SCORE
C. Atkinson	New Beacon	67*
T. Elliott	Newlands	62*
T. Elliott	DPS London	58*
A. Norman	St. Bede's	65
T. Elliott	Ashdown House	61*
C. Munton	Tunbridge Wells BG	72
T. Elliott	King's Canterbury	76

NOTABLE BOWLING PERFORMANCES

PLAYER	OPPOSITION	FIGURES
T. Jenner	King's Rochester	4-3
T. Liddiard	King's Rochester	3-10
C. Munton	Vinehall	4-6
T. Bishop	Whitgift	4-6
C. Munton	Yardley Court	4-30
P. Trevor	King's Canterbury	4-7
C. Munton	Tunbridge Wells BG	5-6

Leaders in the field

Sponsors of the
C&G Cheltenham Cricket Festival
and C&G Trophy

C&G Cheltenham & Gloucester

Cheltenham & Gloucester plc Registered Office: Barnett Way, Gloucester GL4 3RL. Registered in England and Wales No. 2299428.

The best value cricket tours

Please call our specialist playing tours department for a quote when planning your next tour.

Some popular destinations include...

COUNTRY	PRICES FROM	NIGHTS
EUROPE		
Holland	£174	3
South of France	£320	4
Malta	£450	7
Majorca	£390	4
THE CARIBBEAN		
Barbados	£950	7/10/14
Grenada	£850	7/14
St Lucia	£850	7/10/14
St Kitts	£850	7/14
NEW DESTINATION		
St Vincent [combined with another island for 7 days for a 14 day tour]	£950	7
Trinidad & Tobago	£1275	14
WORLDWIDE		
Australia	£1450	14
British Columbia	£1100	10
Dubai	£759	7
Goa	£1100	14
New Zealand	£1450	14
South Africa	£995	10
Sri Lanka	£1050	12
India (Golden Triangle)	£1300	14

Your next step call us on **01684 293175**
or visit www.**gulliversports**.co.uk

Fiddington Manor Tewkesbury Glos GL20 7BJ
email gulliers@gulliversports.co.uk   Fax 01684 297926

ABTA V8321   ATOL 3720   IATA 91201670

GULLIVERS
sports Travel

JOSCA'S

Kingston Road, Frilford, Abingdon, Oxon OX13 5NX

Tel: 01865 391570 Fax: 01865 391042

Email: enquiries@joscas.org.uk

Headmaster: C. Davies   Master i/c Cricket: S. Hibberd

2005 SEASON

Played: 11   Lost: 5   Drawn: 6

Captains: R. Winearls and J. Talbot   Vice-captain: J. Collins

Team selected from: R. Winearls*, J. Talbot*, W. Sensecall,
B. Read, R. Parkin-Mason, J. Collins, H. Gray, E. Yeatman,
E. Howe*, O. Read*, J. Barratt, O. Marples.

SUMMARY

This was a difficult season for the 1st XI, despite having, on paper, what looked like a talented set of players. Against some schools we were unable to chase totals and suffered against teams that bowled good line and length.

Against St. Andrew's we set a competitive 158-4, with good contributions from Ollie Read (36), Will Sensecall (43) and Robbie Winearls (42), but we lacked ideas and variety in our attempt to bowl out the opposition.

Chasing 180 against The Dragon we could have won with another twenty minutes batting after Ollie Read and Jeremy Talbot gave us a fast start.

In our final game against Abingdon we dropped their opener early on and he went on to make a very impressive hundred. Richard Parkin-Mason (54) and Ben Read (13) helped us bat out for the draw.

AVERAGES

BATSMAN	INNINGS	NOT OUT	RUNS	H. SCORE	AVERAGE
R. Parkin-Mason	2	0	66	54	33.0
W. Sensecall	9	2	174	43	24.9
R. Winearls	8	1	165	49*	23.6
O. Read	9	1	171	55	21.4
E. Howe	5	3	39	14*	19.5
J. Talbot	9	1	114	33	14.3

BOWLER	OVERS	MAIDENS	RUNS	WICKETS	AVERAGE
E. Howe	25	4	114	9	12.7
W. Sensecall	29.4	5	144	9	16.0
J. Talbot	31.1	2	131	6	21.8
R. Winearls	29.1	0	127	4	31.7
H. Gray	47	3	193	5	38.6
J. Collins	33.3	1	173	3	57.7

WICKET-KEEPER	PLAYED	CAUGHT	STUMPED
E. Yeatman	10	0	0

NOTABLE BATTING PERFORMANCES

PLAYER	OPPOSITION	SCORE
W. Sensecall	St. Andrew's	43
R. Winearls	St. Andrew's	42
O. Read	Brockhurst	55
R. Winearls	The Dragon	49*
J. Talbot	The Dragon	33
R. Parkin-Mason	Abingdon	54

NOTABLE BOWLING PERFORMANCES

PLAYER	OPPOSITION	FIGURES
E. Howe	St. Hugh's	4-18
H. Gray	St. Andrew's	2-4
W. Sensecall	Brockhurst	4-21
E. Howe	Abingdon	3-6
J. Talbot	Abingdon	2-10

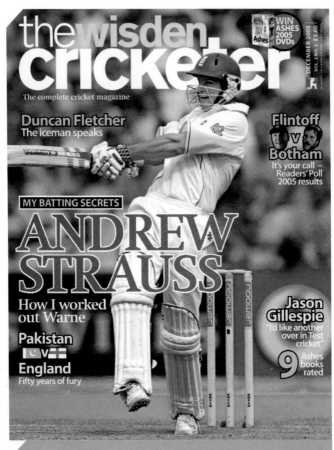

the**wisden** cricketer

The complete cricket magazine

WIN ASHES 2005 DVDs

DECEMBER 2005 VOL. 3 NO. 3 £3.60

Duncan Fletcher
The iceman speaks

Flintoff v Botham
It's your call –
Readers' Poll
2005 results

MY BATTING SECRETS

ANDREW STRAUSS

How I worked
out Warne

Pakistan v England
Fifty years of fury

Jason Gillespie
"I'd like another
over in Test
cricket"

9 Ashes
books
rated

the complete cricket magazine

To order your subscription, call

0870 220 6538

quoting reference SC-ALM01

Specialists in Books, Photographs, Letters and other Sporting Memorabilia

BLOOMSBURY AUCTIONS

Including: Cricket ▪ Angling ▪ Golf ▪ Tennis ▪ Racing ▪ Chess

KEY PLATE TO W.H. MASON'S DRAWING OF A CRICKET MATCH AT **BRIGHTON**, BETWEEN THE **COUNTIES** OF **SUSSEX** & **KENT**.

Descriptive Key to W.H. Mason's National Print of a Cricket Match, 1849.
Realised £4,046

Contact Rupert Powell: rupert@bloomsburyauctions.com for further details

Bloomsbury House | 24 Maddox Street | London | W1S 1PP

T +44 (0) 20 7495 9494 | F +44 (0) 20 7495 9499

info@bloomsburyauctions.com | www.bloomsburyauctions.com

KING'S CANTERBURY

Milner Court, Sturry, Nr. Canterbury, Kent CT2 0AY

Tel: 01227 714000 Fax: 01227 713171

Email: office@junior-kings.co.uk

Headmaster: P.M. Wells Master i/c Cricket: J.R. Gillam

2005 SEASON

Played: 16   Won: 5   Lost: 10   Drawn: 1

Captain: C. MacLeod

Team selected from: C. Macleod*, J. Masters*, T. Dixey*,
N. Evans, J. MacAdam-Stacey, E. Simmons, C. Ovenden,
E. Lundy, T. Chung, N. Hudson-Peacock, D. Winters,
R. Cameron, A. Panda.

Scorer: R. Morley

SUMMARY

It was a tough season for the 1st XI. While they developed as a team and got better as a team as the term went on, they never really hit the heights consistently enough. They lacked penetrative bowling and this made it difficult to exert pressure in the field.

The best performances of the season came against King's Rochester, where Charlie MacLeod and Jack Masters batted magnificently, and against Forest U13, where we witnessed an outstanding fifty from Jack, but more importantly a terrific team batting effort to win the game. The home game against Wellesley (where Tom Dixey hit a fifty) was also a highlight. We were unable to hit a four off the last ball which would have won the game.

The side also attended two hugely enjoyable Twenty20 festivals, at Felsted and Ranby House, where they played some good and entertaining cricket. Charlie MacLeod had a terrific season behind the stumps and steadily improved as captain. The best fielders were Edwin Simmons, Tom Chung, Tom Dixey, Jack Masters and Nick Evans who took many catches and saved many runs. Jack Masters was player of the season.

AVERAGES

BATSMAN	INNINGS	NOT OUT	RUNS	H. SCORE	AVERAGE
J. Masters	16	2	419	88*	29.9
N. Evans	11	3	116	26*	14.5
C. MacLeod	15	0	216	64	14.4
T. Dixey	15	1	169	56	12.1
E. Simmons	14	2	103	19	8.6

BOWLER	OVERS	MAIDENS	RUNS	WICKETS	AVERAGE
J. Masters	83	12	301	27	11.1
T. Chung	33	3	168	11	15.3
D. Winters	28	2	134	7	19.1
T. Dixey	63.4	16	229	12	19.1

WICKET-KEEPER	PLAYED	CAUGHT	STUMPED
C. MacLeod	16	7	6

NOTABLE BATTING PERFORMANCES

PLAYER	OPPOSITION	SCORE
J. Masters	Ranby House	88*
J. Masters	King's Rochester	78
C. MacLeod	King's Rochester	64
T. Dixey	Wellesley House	56
J. Masters	Forest	54
C. MacLeod	Foremarke Hall	51

NOTABLE BOWLING PERFORMANCES

PLAYER	OPPOSITION	FIGURES
J. Masters	King's Rochester	8-3-5-4
J. Masters	St. Lawrence	4-1-8-4
T. Chung	Wellesley House	4-0-13-3
T. Dixey	Holmewood House	5-0-21-3

Normandie à la Carte

Educating Children with a Real Taste of France

Carefully tailored Language and Activity programmes

- Ideal for all types of Schools and Groups
- Courses that motivate and stimulate
- Exclusive use of accommodation

Choose an activity in French from:

Mountain biking - Kayaking - Climbing
High Ropes Course - Sailing - Orienteering

Meet French people:

In the market - At a Goat's Cheese Farm
Walking across the Bay of Mont St. Michel
On the Landing Beaches - Baking croissants
At a Cider Farm

For more information please contact Andrew Caverhill

6 Route des Esnaudières, 50870 Subligny, Normandie, France
Normandie à la Carte is a trading name of European Study Visits Limited.
Reg. in UK No. 3387925

Simply the Best

THE 2005 BOLA 'PROFESSIONAL' CRICKET BOWLING MACHINE

- 12 volt battery or mains operation for use anywhere
- The very latest speed control technology for safety and ease of use
- One mph speed increments for total accuracy
- 28 ball automatic feeder with remote control
- Random delivery mode

IN USE AT ALL EIGHTEEN FIRST CLASS COUNTIES

STUART & WILLIAMS
6 Brookfield Rd, Cotham, Bristol BS6 5PQ
TEL 0117 924 3569. FAX 0117 944 6194
WEBSITE www.bola.co.uk EMAIL info@bola.co.uk

KING'S COLLEGE

West Road, Cambridge, CB3 9DN

Tel: 01223 365814 Fax: 01223 461388

Email: office@kingscam.demon.co.uk

Headmaster: N.J. Robinson Master i/c Cricket: N.G. Lucas

2005 SEASON

Played: 6   Won: 3   Lost: 2   Drawn: 1

Captain: T. Clarke Vice-captain: A. Yandell

Team selected from: T. Clarke*, A. Yandell, D. Wallis, C. Lahr, T. Cowper, T. Obank, H. Hamilton, T. Round, L. Cook, S. Landman, J. Nicholson, J. Firth, T. Norris, H. Naylor.

Scorer: N. Chaudakshetrin

SUMMARY

Another successful season with three victories against King's Ely, Culford and The Leys, achieved with comfortable margins. The two defeats to Bishop's Stortford and St. John's were both against very good teams. Captain Tom Clarke led the team by example with consistently impressive personal performances, with good all-round support by Alex Yandell and Henry Hamilton.

David Wallis and Liam Cook both produced match-winning contributions while Chris Lahr, Theo Cowper and Tom Obank chipped in tellingly at various times. Well done to all.

AVERAGES

BATSMAN	INNINGS	NOT OUT	RUNS	H. SCORE	AVERAGE
T. Clarke	6	1	200	66	40.0
D. Wallis	6	3	63	25	21.0
C. Lahr	3	1	37	32*	18.5
T. Cowper	4	2	34	23*	17.0
T. Obank	5	1	41	20	10.3
H. Hamilton	6	0	61	18	10.2

BOWLER	OVERS	MAIDENS	RUNS	WICKETS	AVERAGE
L. Cook	23	1	99	10	9.9
A. Yandell	22.2	2	87	6	14.5
T. Clarke	32.2	6	102	7	14.6
H. Hamilton	12	2	53	3	17.7
C. Lahr	12	1	64	3	21.3
S, Landman	15	1	90	2	45.0

WICKET-KEEPER	PLAYED	CAUGHT	STUMPED
J. Nicholson	3	0	0
H. Naylor	2	0	0

NOTABLE BATTING PERFORMANCES

PLAYER	OPPOSITION	SCORE
T. Clarke	The Leys	66
T. Clarke	St. John's	42
T. Clarke	Orwell Park	37
T. Clarke	King's Ely	36
C. Lahr	St. John's	32*
D. Wallis	King's Ely	25

NOTABLE BOWLING PERFORMANCES

PLAYER	OPPOSITION	FIGURES
L. Cook	Culford	5-11
T. Clarke	King's Ely	3-7
T. Clarke	The Leys	3-16

The Schools'
CRICKET
ALMANAC
2006

FIRST EDITION

Edited by Grenville Simons
and Andrew Fraser

Foreword by Christopher Martin-Jenkins

Featuring contributions by
Ian Botham OBE, Clare Connor OBE,
Dr David English MBE, Nick Gandon,
Jack Russell MBE

A record of U18 school cricket for the 2005 season

Further details and copies available from: The Editors, Wisteria Books,
Wisteria Cottage, Birt Street, Birtsmorton, Malvern, Worcs WR13 6AW
Tel/fax - 01684 833578 Email - sca@wisteriabooks.co.uk
www.wisteriabooks.co.uk

PORTRAIT OF A CRICKETING SCHOOLMASTER

Raymond Charles Robertson-Glasgow (1901 - 1965)
Oxford University and Somerset

by Andrew Fraser

'It was a chilly, misty afternoon, and I was filled with vivid apprehensions. The taxi stopped in front of a huge red-brick building, its turrets and steep-pitched roofs reminiscent of some fairy-tale castle. On the grass in the middle of the drive I saw a group of perhaps half a dozen boys, all considerably larger and older than me, and towering above them, wearing tweed plus-fours and two or three thick jerseys, a colossal, jolly man, a very jovial giant, who was even more absorbed in the game they were playing than the boys around him. Each was armed with a conker on a string, but instead of doing traditional battle with these, they were using them as missiles - whirling them round and round in accelerating, vertical circles and then releasing them, their evident purpose to send them clear over the rooftops and turrets that towered above. The giant was the only one achieving this to a background of encouraging shouts and cheers and laughter.'

Such was the first meeting of former pupil, John Maurice, with R.C. Robertson-Glasgow, and there are few who met him without fond memories. Affable and entertaining, he loved cricket almost as much as he loved people and wrote about both with wit and affection. He combined the carefree nature of a schoolboy with the insight and prose of Arlott or Cardus. He is most famed for his writings on cricket, both in the press and as an author, but there was more to 'Crusoe' than a talented wordsmith. He was a first-rate opening bowler for Oxford University and Somerset, from 1920 to 1937, playing in four successive Varsity matches from 1920 to 1923. He took 464 wickets at 25.77 and was, for a while, in the minds of the England selectors. In 1924 he took 9-38 at Lords against

Middlesex, his best bowling analysis, and later that summer was selected for the Gentlemen v Players. In 1930 he played for an England XI against Australia, playing alongside Hammond, Ames and Tate against Woodfull, Grimmett and Bradman. As with his writing, he refused to take cricket too seriously, and perhaps thereby did not help his England prospects. 'In the age of the specialist he remained the true amateur. He played games for fun and never forgot that a game is just that.'

Throughout his life, when journalism did not pay all his bills, he was a schoolmaster; in the early years at his old prep school, St. Edmund's Hindhead, and later at a school founded by his elder brother, St. Andrew's Prep School, Pangbourne. His own boarding school experiences, far away from his parents, gave him a warmth and understanding that set him aside from many of his colleagues, especially during the war years. His untimely death in 1965 robbed the world of a man who still had much to give. Leonard Crawley summed it up in the 'Field':

'He was much the nicest man I have ever met. He loved life and he loved people. In him there was a deeply Christian trait which insisted that he made the humblest minds of the humblest people happy in his brilliant company.'

Ray and his older brother Bobs were born in Scotland and sent to boarding school in Surrey. His own accounts of life at school are littered with tales of old-fashioned naughtiness mixed with the melancholy and loneliness of boarding life at the time. The headmaster's sister related how arrangements for the two boys at the end of term were always uncertain and that on occasions they would remain at school throughout the holidays! From St. Edmund's he went on to Charterhouse where he opened the batting and bowling, and then to Oxford where he was in his element, spending far more time at The Parks than at his studies. While still at Corpus he began his teaching at St Edmunds, where he was adored by the boys and staff alike. 'He was on intimate terms with everyone, from the most insignificant boy to the cook, gardener, or handyman' and his cricketing exploits were followed by all in the newspapers.

It is no surprise that many remember him for his eccentricity as well as his kindness. The school Chronicle of 1935 reported that '... on July 15th Mr. R.C. Robertson-Glasgow fell into the swimming pool and declared it open'. At St. Andrew's, where he was affectionately known as 'Corney', he would regularly perform at the end of term 'Sing-Song', when he could be relied upon to dominate every chorus and split sides, including his own, with his solos. He founded the school Literary Society and at the outbreak of war joined the Home Guard, of which he told and wrote hilarious accounts. Many of these, along with humerous anecdotes of a day's teaching, would lighten the atmosphere in the staff room or over dinner, especially during the darkest days of the war. He was always fond of lavatorial humour, even in the press box, and found great amusement in mischevious bouts of flatulence.

In the address at his funeral, his humility and deep love of the game at its most simple level were summed up:

'... for all his distinction at cricket and his wide acquaintance with the great men of the sporting world Raymond's first love was for the humbler games, village and prep school cricket, and unofficial 'Test Matches' in the back garden. To him almost every person was of interest, and cricket was to him above all concerned with people.'

Perhaps he was, like so many of the best teachers, the schoolboy who never quite grew up.

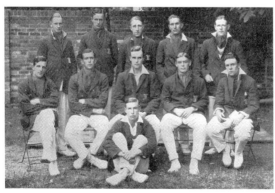

Oxford University XI, 1922 - R.C. Robertson-Glasgow is standing second from the left

KING'S ELY

Ely, Cambridgeshire CB7 4DB

Tel: 01353 660753 Fax: 01353 665281

Email: DavidB@kings-ely.cambs.sch.uk

Headmaster: A. J. Duncan   Master i/c Cricket: Dr S. Robinson

2005 SEASON

Played: 9   Won: 3   Lost: 6

Captain: T. Pitfield

Team selected from: N. Pope*, J. Lines*, T. Pitfield*,
S. Saxby*, J. Turner, L. Cunnah*, C. Baker*, L. Saunders*,
J. Powell*, A. Harris, J. East.

SUMMARY

The season started promisingly with a high-scoring game
against Oundle. Although the game was lost, some encouraging
scores were posted. Disappointingly, the positive signs from the
first game soon dissipated as the team slumped to six successive
defeats. There were some bright moments amidst the gloom!
Nick Pope was showing promise with the bat and Tom Pitfield
and James Turner were returning reasonably economical
bowling figures.

Overall, though, the trouble seemed to be the bowlers'
inability to restrict the opposition total to one that could be
chased. When a target was achievable, however, the batting
seemed to crumble.

The arrival of a professional coach seemed to remedy some
of the problems, and the team won the last three games of the
season by comfortable margins.

AVERAGES

BATSMAN	INNINGS	NOT OUT	RUNS	H. SCORE	AVERAGE
N. Pope	9	1	128	62	16.0
T. Pitfield	9	1	97	29	12.1
J. Lines	9	0	101	29	11.2
J. Turner	9	3	57	16*	9.5
L. Cunnah	9	3	45	14*	7.5

BOWLER	OVERS	MAIDENS	RUNS	WICKETS	AVERAGE
T. Pitfield	62	11	166	15	11.1
J. Turner	60	9	183	16	11.4
J. Lines	42	1	153	9	17.0
L. Cunnah	50	4	149	7	21.3

WICKET-KEEPER	PLAYED	CAUGHT	STUMPED
N. Pope	9	0	3

NOTABLE BATTING PERFORMANCES

PLAYER	OPPOSITION	SCORE
N. Pope	Wellingborough	62
N. Pope	Deacon School	37*

NOTABLE BOWLING PERFORMANCES

PLAYER	OPPOSITION	FIGURES
T. Pitfield	King's College Cambridge	8-1-19-4
J. Turner	Woodbridge	5-3-5-2
J. Lines	Culford	4-0-5-4
T. Pitfield	Culford	6-3-7-3

LOCKERS PARK

Lockers Park Lane, Hemel Hempstead, Hertfordshire HP1 1TL
Tel: 01442 251712 Fax: 01442 234150
Email: secretary@lockerspark.herts.sch.uk
Headmaster: D. Lees-Jones   Master i/c Cricket: S. Gowing

2005 SEASON

Played: 8   Won: 4   Lost: 3   Drawn: 1

Captain: B. Cooper

Team selected from: B. Hatt, C. Brewer, B. Cooper*, J. Moore,
L. Frey, T. Smith, K. Amin, C. McPhail, L. Newsum, O. Young,
L. Stuart-Smith, M. Rasiah, J. Olley.

SUMMARY

Like the weather, the season started in unpredictable fashion,
but the batting of captain Ben Cooper proved to be the
consistent factor of the summer as he averaged just under 60.
Following a disappointing start, the team were inspired by a
Twenty20 trip to Lords. Chris Brewer made 79 and Cooper 68*
in a 25 run victory over Beechwood Park. The fast flow of runs
continued at 12 per over, with victory over Westbrook Hay.
Brewer (45) shared a 121 run partnership with Cooper, whose
fine innings of 98* had spectators moving their cars as he hit 13
fours and 5 sixes.

The season closed with a thrilling run chase against York
House. Set 161 to win off 23 overs, Ben Hatt and Cooper struck
18 fours and 2 sixes in a partnership of 121 off 10 overs. Hatt
remained unbeaten on 71, including 2 sixes and three lost balls
to seal victory in just 19.5 overs.

The fact that four batsmen scored over 800 runs underlines
where the team's strength lay this year. Credit goes to all the
boys, however, and they genuinely enjoyed their cricket.

AVERAGES

BATSMAN	INNINGS	NOT OUT	RUNS	H. SCORE	AVERAGE
B. Cooper	8	2	352	98*	58.7
B. Hatt	8	1	186	71*	26.6
C. Brewer	8	0	162	78	20.3
J. Moore	8	0	144	34	18.0

BOWLER	OVERS	MAIDENS	RUNS	WICKETS	AVERAGE
O. Young	35	3	143	11	13.0
K. Amin	34	4	168	8	21.0
L. Newsum	42	2	203	9	22.6

WICKET-KEEPER	PLAYED	CAUGHT	STUMPED
L. Frey	8	3	1

NOTABLE BATTING PERFORMANCES

PLAYER	OPPOSITION	SCORE
B. Cooper	Westbrook Hay	98*
B. Cooper	The Beacon	62
B. Cooper	Beechwood Park	68*
B. Cooper	Westbrook Hay	46
C. Brewer	Beechwood Park	78
B. Hatt	York House	71*
C. Brewer	Westbrook Hay	45

NOTABLE BOWLING PERFORMANCES

PLAYER	OPPOSITION	FIGURES
O. Young	Edge Grove	3-32
K. Amin	Westbrook Hay	3-11
L. Newsum	The Beacon	3-39

LORETTO

North High Street, Musselburgh, East Lothian EH21 6JA

Tel: 0131 653 4574 Fax: 0131 653 4571

Email: pearced@loretto.com

Headmaster: R.G. Selley   Master i/c Cricket: D.H. Pearce

2005 SEASON

Played: 7   Won: 5   Lost: 2

Captain: A. Mackay   Vice-captain: A. Wilson

Team selected from: H. Fisher, R. Paterson, A. Mackay, A. Wilson, A. Buchanan-Smith, G. Wilson, G. Marriott, H. Marriott, J. Allan, E. Dudgeon, C. Manders, C. Allan, A. Barclay, D. Cowe.

SUMMARY

Our most successful season for several years started with a record 30 over score against Cargilfield with Henry Fisher blasting a super 94*, another season's best. Wins followed against St. Mary's, Melrose, Strathallan, Craigclowan and Ardvreck, with our two losses to Belhaven and Fettes.

This team played beyond expectation and in the bowling department Alex Mackay led the way with able support from Ross Paterson, Conor Manders and Archie Wilson. Alex Mackay took a splendid 6-15 at Fettes. On the batting front Henry Fisher, Archie Wilson and Angus Buchanan-Smith made valuable runs.

A super lot to coach and perhaps the highlight of the season was the visit to the Scotland v Sussex game where we were treated to a leg-spin masterclass from Mustaq Ahmed on a glorious Scottish summer's afternoon.

AVERAGES

BATSMAN	INNINGS	NOT OUT	RUNS	H. SCORE	AVERAGE
H. Fisher	7	2	171	94*	34.2
J. Allan	3	2	28	17*	28.0
A. Wilson	7	2	120	60*	24.0
A. Buchanan-Smith	5	2	63	47*	21.0

BOWLER	OVERS	MAIDENS	RUNS	WICKETS	AVERAGE
A. Mackay	35	12	80	20	4.0
A. Wilson	17	3	33	8	4.1
C. Manders	19	4	42	6	7.0
R. Paterson	36	8	104	14	7.4

WICKET-KEEPER	PLAYED	CAUGHT	STUMPED
J. Allan	7	5	0

NOTABLE BATTING PERFORMANCES

PLAYER	OPPOSITION	SCORE
H. Fisher	Cargilfield	94*
A. Wilson	St. Mary's	60*
A. Buchanan-Smith	Strathallan	47*
R. Paterson	Craigclowan	30*
H. Fisher	Ardvreck	43*

NOTABLE BOWLING PERFORMANCES

PLAYER	OPPOSITION	FIGURES
A. Mackay	Fettes	6-15
A. Mackay	Cargilfield	4-8
R. Paterson	Cargilfield	3-18
A. Mackay	Riley	3-4

MILLFIELD

Edgarley Hall, Glastonbury, Somerset BA6 8LD
Tel: 01458 837575 Fax: 01458 833679
Email: office@millfieldprep.com

Headmaster: K.A. Cheney   Master i/c Cricket: Chris Twort

2005 SEASON

Played: 24   Won: 16   Lost: 5   Drawn: 3

Captain: N. Pang   Vice-captain: T. Galpin

Team selected from: N. Pang*, T. Galpin*, T. Moore*,
F. Bullough*, F. Walker*, T. King*, D. Bell-Drummond,
H. Ellison, B. Hetherington, T. Lett, J. Dowsett, J. Royall,
J. Allan, M. Ward, M. Pearson, C. Lambden, G. Taylor.

Scorer: Simon Wynn

SUMMARY

Highlight of the season was the assured batting of eleven-year-old Daniel Bell-Drummond (a regular in Kent's U14 side). As well as his 629 runs for the 1st XI, he also scored six centuries for the U12 side.

The national JET Shield for prep schools was retained. Daniel and Harry Ellison put on 77 in the final against Dulwich College Prep. The county U13 Shield was won for the seventh year running - skipper Nick Pang and Daniel putting on an unbroken 200 for the second wicket. In the David English/Bunbury Cup we were defeated in the semi-final at the hands of the eventual winners, Whitgift.

Two South African prep schools, The Ridge and Waterkloof House, were hosted and the annual short tour of Devon and Cornwall took place as usual. The 2006 side will rely on the experience of Daniel and Harry, and will be bolstered by a number of this years highly successful colts, who were winners of the national eight-a-side hardball competition.

AVERAGES

BATSMAN	INNINGS	NOT OUT	RUNS	H. SCORE	AVERAGE
D. Bell-Drummond	18	8	629	102*	62.9
N. Pang	21	4	583	103*	34.3
T. Moore	18	3	466	131*	31.1
T. Galpin	20	6	407	67*	29.1
F. Walker	14	1	193	38	14.8
F. Bullough	13	3	144	26	14.4

BOWLER	OVERS	MAIDENS	RUNS	WICKETS	AVERAGE
D. Bell-Drummond	36.1	4	122	11	11.1
N. Pang	157	25	488	40	12.2
T. King	106.3	14	367	29	12.7
B. Hetherington	56	4	226	14	16.1
F. Bullough	95	8	348	20	17.4
H. Ellison	52.4	5	192	8	24.0

WICKET-KEEPER	PLAYED	CAUGHT	STUMPED
F. Walker	22	11	9
T. Moore	24	2	0

NOTABLE BATTING PERFORMANCES

PLAYER	OPPOSITION	SCORE
T. Moore	Mid-Glamorgan U13	131*
N. Pang	Taunton Prep	103*
D. Bell-Drummond	Monkton Combe	102*
T. Moore	Cornwall U13	97
D. Bell-Drummond	Taunton Prep	96*
D. Bell-Drummond	The Ridge (South Africa)	79*
T. Moore	Cranmore	72

NOTABLE BOWLING PERFORMANCES

PLAYER	OPPOSITION	FIGURES
N. Pang	Chafyn Grove	3-1-6-5
N. Pang	Sherborne	5-1-21-5
F. Bullough	Writhlington	4-1-6-4
T. King	Beechen Cliff	4-0-11-4
D. Bell-Drummond	Cranmore	8.2-2-15-4
T. Galpin	Monkton Combe	6-0-19-4
N. Pang	Millfield U14 'B'	7-0-24-4

MONKTON COMBE

Combe Down, Bath, BA2 7ET

Tel: 01225 831217 Fax: 01225 840312

Email: sport@monktonjunior.org.uk

Headmaster: C. Stafford Master i/c Cricket: A. Parnell

2005 SEASON

Played: 13   Won: 7   Lost: 4   Drawn: 2

Captain: T. Davies   Vice-captains: E. Vickers and E. Borton

Team selected from: T. Davies, E. Borton, B. Harris, E. Vickers,
J. Ford, M. Paynter, S. Florentiades, W. Dabell, T. Cushnir,
D. Newport, C. French, W. Graves, O. Willder, A. Martin,
P. Shipp, O. Millard, B. Hallé.

Scorer: D. Symonds

SUMMARY

A very successful season from a team that always gave
everything. The batting was dominated by Vickers and Davies
but many others provided some good cameos.

Bowling was not always at its tightest, but catches were held
and stumps hit. Good wins against all the local schools and
victory again in the County Cup were definite highlights, as
were Vickers' powerful hitting against All Hallows, Clifton and
Bristol GS.

The side will undoubtedly be weaker next year, but a few
Year 7s were 'blooded' and should provide a good score for
2006.

AVERAGES

BATSMAN	INNINGS	NOT OUT	RUNS	H. SCORE	AVERAGE
E. Vickers	12	5	351	56*	50.1
T. Davies	12	4	284	54	35.5
B. Harris	6	2	81	22	20.3
E. Borton	12	2	113	31*	11.3
M. Paynter	7	0	73	31	10.4

BOWLER	OVERS	MAIDENS	RUNS	WICKETS	AVERAGE
B. Hallé	49	10	163	19	8.6
E. Vickers	48	2	153	14	10.9
B. Harris	51	5	230	13	17.7
T. Davies	60	7	223	12	18.6
M. Paynter	50	6	223	12	18.6

WICKET-KEEPER	PLAYED	CAUGHT	STUMPED
S. Florentiades	12	3	2

NOTABLE BATTING PERFORMANCES

PLAYER	OPPOSITION	SCORE
E. Vickers	All Hallows	56*
T. Davies	Sandroyd	54
T. Davies	Hazlegrove	47*
T. Davies	Prior Park	46*
E. Vickers	Bristol GS	43*

NOTABLE BOWLING PERFORMANCES

PLAYER	OPPOSITION	FIGURES
B. Hallé	Warminster	5-8
B. Hallé	Chipping Campden	4-6
E. Vickers	Bristol GS	4-8

MOOR PARK

Moor Park, Ludlow, Shropshire SY8 4DZ

Tel: 01584 872342 Fax: 01584 877311

Email: head@moorpark.shropshire.sch.uk

Headmaster: M Piercy Master i/c Cricket: J. Martin

2005 SEASON

Played: 9 Won: 6 Lost: 2 Drawn: 1

Captain: R. Salmon Vice-captain: B. Bradley

Team selected from: R. Salmon*, B. Bradley*, J. Price*,
W. Burton, P. Wild, H. de Haan, E. Harwood, H. Jones,
H. Brentall, C. Davies, L. Cowling, T. Maitland, W. Brandon.

SUMMARY

On paper, the 2005 side looked experienced and expectations were high, and the team did not disappoint. The performances on the field were exceptional, and although Rupert Salmon as captain, remained the rock in the side throughout the season, there were many other notable performances.

By the time the team came across Bishops Hereford they were in full flight and playing some very impressive cricket. Bishops had six county players, but having put them into bat, they simply could not get our bowlers away. The comment made by their coach was that it had been one of the best U13 bowling performances he had ever seen - quite a compliment. Our batsmen then set about reaching the target and we claimed another very worthy victory.

The team lost only two games in total, one of which was against an U14 Shrewsbury team who were simply too old and too good for our Year 7s and 8s. During the second half of the term there was less cricket than we would have liked due to the weather, but the team had a superb season. Rupert Salmon captained the side extremely well.

AVERAGES

BATSMAN	INNINGS	NOT OUT	RUNS	H. SCORE	AVERAGE
R. Salmon	8	2	239	69	39.8
B. Bradley	8	2	110	38*	18.3
J. Price	8	1	104	48*	14.9

BOWLER	OVERS	MAIDENS	RUNS	WICKETS	AVERAGE
J. Price	52.1	6	121	22	5.5
R. Salmon	60.4	15	121	15	8.1
B. Bradley	60	6	177	13	13.6

WICKET-KEEPER	PLAYED	CAUGHT	STUMPED
W. Burton	8	4	2

NOTABLE BATTING PERFORMANCES

PLAYER	OPPOSITION	SCORE
R. Salmon	St. Richard's	69
J. Price	Hillstone	48*
R. Salmon	Packwood Haugh	58

NOTABLE BOWLING PERFORMANCES

PLAYER	OPPOSITION	FIGURES
J. Price	St. Richard's	8-2-11-4
J. Price	St. Richard's	9-1-15-4
R. Salmon	Winterfold	7-4-5-4

THE NEW BEACON

Brittains Lane, Sevenoaks, Kent TN13 2PB
Tel: 01732 452131 Fax: 01732 459509
Email: admin@newbeacon.kent.sch.uk

Headmaster: R. Constantine Master i/c Cricket: I.C. Buchanan-Dunlop

2005 SEASON

Played: 12   Won: 8   Drawn: 4

Captain: H. Galpin Vice-captain: S. Clark

Team selected from: H. Galpin*, S. Clark*, R. Dunnett*,
M. Murray*, C. Watson*, S. Harris*, C. Carver*, G. Cantlay*,
A. Gill*, T. Brown*, H. Horner*, H. Elliott*.

Scorer: Jack Brewster*

SUMMARY

The New Beacon 1st XI had an excellent season, winning eight
games and drawing four.

The highlight of the season was beating a Kent XI by five
wickets. This was a wonderful team performance. We restricted
Kent to 107-9 off 35 overs. We used seven bowlers, including
two spinners. All the bowlers bowled very well, with great
variation. They were well supported with some first-class
ground fielding and catching by the whole team. After this
fielding display, the batsman's job was made much easier, and
they knocked off the runs comfortably for the loss of only five
wickets and nine overs to spare, Harry Galpin making forty-
seven.

Special mention should be made of Harry Galpin who
captained the side very well all season, and contributed greatly
in every game; also Andrew Gill, Mark Murray, Sam Harris and
Sandy Clark, who all made major contributions during this
highly successful season. This team always played highly
exciting and attacking cricket. Well done.

AVERAGES

BATSMAN	INNINGS	NOT OUT	RUNS	H. SCORE	AVERAGE
H. Galpin	12	5	474	91	67.7
M. Murray	10	7	135	25	45.0
S. Clark	9	3	214	69*	35.7
C. Watson	12	2	307	96	30.7
R. Dunnett	10	2	174	67*	21.8

BOWLER	OVERS	MAIDENS	RUNS	WICKETS	AVERAGE
S. Harris	44	8	130	18	7.2
A. Gill	38	8	110	14	7.9
S. Clark	31	4	97	9	10.8
M. Murray	33	3	80	5	16.0
H. Galpin	33	3	106	6	17.7
T. Brown	33.4	3	121	6	20.2

WICKET-KEEPER	PLAYED	CAUGHT	STUMPED
R. Dunnett	12	7	2

NOTABLE BATTING PERFORMANCES

PLAYER	OPPOSITION	SCORE
H. Galpin	Dulwich	91
H. Galpin	Holmewood House	80*
C. Watson	Sevenoaks	96
S. Clark	Yardley	69*
R. Dunnett	Solefield	67*

NOTABLE BOWLING PERFORMANCES

PLAYER	OPPOSITION	FIGURES
S. Harris	Rose Hill	7-9
H. Elliott	Kent XI	4-15

NEWLANDS

Eastbourne Road, Seaford, East Sussex BN25 4NP
Tel: 01323 892344 Fax: 01323 898420
Email: newlands@msn.com
Headmaster: O. Price   Master i/c Cricket: Colin Wells

2005 SEASON

Played: 10   Won: 6   Lost: 3   Drawn: 1

Captain: C. Holland   Vice-captain: T. Donovan

Team selected from: C. Holland*, T. Donovan, O. Smith,
M. Hobden, S. Radford, A. Price, H. Buckland, A. Lally,
S. Bennett, M. Brown, B. Smith.

Scorer: T. Hurst

SUMMARY

The strongest 1st XI for a few years had a successful season
under the coaching of ex-county and international cricketer
Colin Wells.

The batting was a good balance of attack and defence, with
Matthew Hobden being the most consistent performer, Oliver
Smith the most stylish and Harry Buckland the most improved.

Bowling was generally good and the length and line
improved as the season progressed. The lone spinner, Alex
Price, deserved far more wickets. County seamer Oliver Smith
was consistently threatening and Matthew Hobden had the most
victims. Aaron Lally was the most improved bowler.

The fielding was of a high standard. Skipper Craig Holland
led the way with some superb catching and both ground-
fielding and throwing improved. The wicket-keeper, Spencer
Bennett, became very proficient.

AVERAGES

BATSMAN	INNINGS	NOT OUT	RUNS	H. SCORE	AVERAGE
M. Hobden	9	2	253	64	36.1
H. Buckland	5	2	79	38	26.3
O. Smith	10	2	158	52	19.8
A. Price	9	0	164	39	18.2
C. Holland	6	0	78	17	13.0
S. Radford	6	0	66	6	11.0

BOWLER	OVERS	MAIDENS	RUNS	WICKETS	AVERAGE
O. Smith	-	-	97	14	6.9
M. Hobden	-	-	138	15	9.2
T. Donovan	-	-	44	4	11.0
A. Lally	-	-	92	7	13.1
S. Radford	-	-	43	3	14.3
C. Holland	-	-	144	10	14.4

WICKET-KEEPER	PLAYED	CAUGHT	STUMPED
S. Bennett	10	3	0

NOTABLE BATTING PERFORMANCES

PLAYER	OPPOSITION	SCORE
M. Hobden	Claremont	60*
M. Hobden	St. Christopher's	58
O. Smith	St. Christopher's	52
M. Hobden	St. Bede's	64

NOTABLE BOWLING PERFORMANCES

PLAYER	OPPOSITION	FIGURES
M. Hobden	St. Christopher's	4-13
O. Smith	Claremont	3-2

NORTHAMPTON

Great Houghton Hall, Great Houghton, Northampton NN4 7AG

Tel: 01604 761907 Fax: 01604 761251

Email: office@northamptonschool.com

Headmaster: R. Barnes   Master i/c Cricket: P. Bates

2005 SEASON

Played: 9   Won: 2   Lost: 4   Drawn: 3

Captain: C. Smart   Vice-captain: W. Dunkley

Team selected from: S. Foster*, L. Sarkeshik, C. Hill*,
C. Smart*, C. Knowles, W. Dunkley*, M. Farquhar, A. Morton,
S. Crosby-Browne, A. Graham, M. Graham,
W. Shires, H. Elkington.

SUMMARY

A season of mixed fortunes in terms of results, but many excellent performances. There were pleasing victories over Spratton and Oundle, and draws with Arnold, Swanbourne and Wellingborough. We were defeated by Winchester House, Bilton, Maidwell and Loughborough GS in the U13 Bunbury Trophy.

The outstanding batsman was Seb Foster whose 284 runs at 35.5 played a major part in our season. His technique, timing and temperament were a pleasure to observe. Chris Smart, our captain and opening bowler, proved very consistent with his left-arm pace. He returned several fine performances and led by committed example. Will Dunkley produced some vey good all-round efforts. His 50* versus Loughborough GS and 5-53 with his leg-spin against Wellingborough were outstanding. Charlie Knowles produced some excellent fielding and his 4-14 versus Spratton was especially admirable.

The improvement and development of the side provided much pleasure, Charlie Hill's maiden half-century (52*) in the final match against Maidwell Hall being but one example.

AVERAGES

BATSMAN	INNINGS	NOT OUT	RUNS	H. SCORE	AVERAGE
S. Foster	9	1	284	66*	35.5
C. Hill	9	4	129	52*	25.8
W. Dunkley	8	2	135	50*	22.5
C. Smart	8	0	141	45	17.6
A. Morton	5	0	45	28	9.0

BOWLER	OVERS	MAIDENS	RUNS	WICKETS	AVERAGE
C. Knowles	12	1	56	4	14.0
W. Shires	11	0	66	4	16.5
W. Dunkley	26	3	143	7	20.4
M. Farquhar	39	4	154	7	22.0
S. Crosby-Browne	31.1	6	104	4	26.0
C. Smart	53	11	189	7	27.0

WICKET-KEEPER	PLAYED	CAUGHT	STUMPED
S. Foster	5	3	0
L. Sarkeshik	4	0	2

NOTABLE BATTING PERFORMANCES

PLAYER	OPPOSITION	SCORE
S. Foster	Arnold Lodge	62
W. Dunkley	Loughborough GS	50*
S. Foster	Winchester House	58
S. Foster	Oundle	66*
C. Hill	Maidwell Hall	52*
C. Smart	Spratton	45
C. Smart	Swanbourne	37

NOTABLE BOWLING PERFORMANCES

PLAYER	OPPOSITION	FIGURES
C. Knowles	Spratton	3-1-14-4
W. Dunkley	Wellingborough	12-1-53-5
C. Smart	Swanbourne	8-0-25-2
M. Farquhar	Bilton Grange	7-0-23-2
M. Farquhar	Oundle	6-1-18-2
C. Smart	Oundle ·	6-0-11-2
W. Shires	Oundle	2-0-14-2

NORTHBOURNE PARK

Betteshanger, Deal, Kent CT14 0NW

Tel: 01304 611215 Fax: 01304 619020

Email: riley@northbournepark.com

Headmaster: S. Sides   Master i/c Cricket: C. Riley

2005 SEASON

Played: 7   Won: 6   Lost: 1

Captain: A. Higson

Team selected from: A. Higson*, A. Furneaux, F. Haffenden, H. Hamilton, T. Rook, M. Jay, S. Staunton, M. Mejanes, B. Kemp*, V. Chaudhuri*, M. Linington, C. Hart, L. Burrell, J. Cunningham, H. Tresidder.

Scorer: J. Cunningham

SUMMARY

This year the 1st XI was made up of a good mixture of Year 7 and Year 8 boys. What an incredible season it was for all concerned. We started off by winning our first game rather convincingly and continued to play some fantastic cricket. The boys' natural talent was not the only aspect on which they relied for their success. The team worked hard in the nets, on both their batting and bowling techniques, and were rewarded for all the extra effort and dedication. Special mention must go to Alex Higson and Vikram Chaudhuri who consistently led from the front in the batting department, with some mature, stunning and calculated strokeplay. The others responded in a most positive fashion, batting around them and contributing greatly to every innings.

In the bowling department, Vikram, Alex, Ben Kemp, Matthew Jay and Max Linington all bowled with great guile, intelligence and accuracy, limiting the opposition to less than 100 runs in every game. The boys fielded well, especially Angus Furneaux, who was excellent behind the stumps. It has been a pleasure to coach such an enthusiastic group of cricketers and I wish them all the very best in the future.

AVERAGES

BATSMAN	INNINGS	NOT OUT	RUNS	H. SCORE	AVERAGE
V. Chaudhuri	6	3	117	58*	39.0
A. Higson	5	3	68	35*	34.0

BOWLER	OVERS	MAIDENS	RUNS	WICKETS	AVERAGE
M. Linington	13.1	4	33	15	2.2
A. Higson	31	9	59	15	3.9
V. Chaudhuri	30	5	89	15	5.9
B. Kemp	33	7	85	13	6.5
M. Jay	26.5	2	92	9	10.2

WICKET-KEEPER	PLAYED	CAUGHT	STUMPED
A. Furneaux	-	-	-

NOTABLE BATTING PERFORMANCES

PLAYER	OPPOSITION	SCORE
V. Chaudhuri	Wellesley House	58*
V. Chaudhuri	King's Canterbury JS	32*
A. Furneaux	King's Canterbury JS	23
A. Higson	Wellesley House	35*

NOTABLE BOWLING PERFORMANCES

PLAYER	OPPOSITION	FIGURES
A. Higson	Eastcourt	5-3-4-8
V. Chaudhuri	St. Edmund's	6-1-21-5
M. Linington	Wellesley House	5-1-21-5
M. Linington	King's Canterbury JS	3-0-6-4
M. Jay	King's Canterbury JS	4-0-14-4
B. Kemp	King's Canterbury JS	5-1-10-4
M. Linington	Wellesley House	3-1-2-3

NORTHCOTE LODGE

26 Bolingbroke Grove, London, SW11 6EL

Tel: 020 8682 8880 Fax: 020 8682 8879

Email: g.hughes@northwoodschools.com

Headmaster: P. Cheeseman Master i/c Cricket: Graham Hughes

2005 SEASON

Played: 6   Won: 3   Drawn: 3

Captain: W. Rosier   Vice-captain: M. Thurlow

Team selected from: W. Rosier*, O. Feather*,
G. Bedford-Russell*, A. Kidwell*, M. Thurlow*, W. Ayrton,
O. Logan, M. Wright, M. Sarre, N. Salmon, H. Zundel.

Scorer: W. Dearman

SUMMARY

This is one of the best 1st XI teams for a while. We were all upset to have three matches rained off. The side batted well every game with totals of 150 in easy reach. Our big totals were mainly due to William Rosier, George Bedford-Russell and the magnificent Oliver Feather whose batting was a pleasure to watch.

Two of the three matches that we drew, we should have won, but failed to bowl the opposition out. Alexander Kidwell and Max Thurlow were the pick of the seven bowlers, and Matthew Sarre not only bowled his leg-spin well but his catching and fielding overall were amazing.

We were ably led by William Rosier and Max Thurlow.

AVERAGES

BATSMAN	INNINGS	NOT OUT	RUNS	H. SCORE	AVERAGE
A. Kidwell	3	2	79	50*	79.0
O. Feather	6	2	277	78*	69.3
G. Bedford-Russell	5	2	99	31*	33.0
W. Rosier	5	1	122	52*	30.5
W. Ayrton	5	0	42	23	8.4
O. Logan	4	0	26	12	6.5

BOWLER	OVERS	MAIDENS	RUNS	WICKETS	AVERAGE
H. Zundel	10	0	52	5	10.4
A. Kidwell	31	7	101	9	11.2
M. Wright	8	0	62	5	12.4
M. Sarre	24.1	4	111	8	13.9
M. Thurlow	28	5	107	7	15.3
N. Salmon	16	2	67	4	16.7

WICKET-KEEPER	PLAYED	CAUGHT	STUMPED
O. Logan	4	2	1
W. Rosier	2	0	0

NOTABLE BATTING PERFORMANCES

PLAYER	OPPOSITION	SCORE
O. Feather	Tower House	56
O. Feather	Shrewsbury House 2nd XI	75*
O. Feather	Rokeby 2nd XI	78*
W. Rosier	Eaton House	52*
A. Kidwell	Thomas's Clapham	50*
G. Bedford-Russell	Shrewsbury House 2nd XI	31*

NOTABLE BOWLING PERFORMANCES

PLAYER	OPPOSITION	FIGURES
O. Feather	Thomas's Clapham	2-2
H. Zundel	Eaton House	2-10
M. Wright	Thomas's Clapham	2-8
A. Kidwell	Dulwich College 2nd XI	3-15
M. Thurlow	Shrewsbury House 2nd XI	2-18
M. Thurlow	Eaton House	2-10
M. Sarre	Rokeby 2nd XI	5-26

NORTHWOOD

Moor Farm, Sandy Lodge Road, Rickmansworth, Herts WD3 1LW

Tel: 01923 825648 Fax: 01923 835802

Email: northwoodprep1@hotmail.com

Headmaster: T.D. Lee   Master i/c Cricket: M. Griggs

2005 SEASON

Played: 3   Won: 3

Captain: I. Shah

SUMMARY

The 2005 season was frustratingly reduced to only three matches unaffected by the weather. This was all the more galling considering that we were fortunate enough to have an extremely strong squad of players this season, a number of whom had performed well the previous year in the first team.

One of these boys, Ishan Shah, was our thoughtful and skilful captain and led the team to victory in all three of our completed matches. He dominated the batting in one particular match against St. John's, to such an extent that numerous school records were annihilated in one fell swoop. In a total of 210-6 from the allotted 30 overs, Ishan's incredible contribution of 145* contained 21 fours and 7 sixes, and he only came to the crease in the third over of our innings. Our opponents impressively fell only 32 runs short in their reply, and they deserve much credit for their resolve.

Also worthy of note was the contribution of two bowlers who were in Year 7 at the time, Jayant Pindolia (including a metronomic spell of 2-12 off 6 overs in the high-scoring St. John's match) and Vishnu Nambiar, whose seven wickets cost just 7.6 runs each.

AVERAGES

BATSMAN	INNINGS	NOT OUT	RUNS	H. SCORE	AVERAGE
I. Shah	2	1	163	145*	163.0
M. Sinderberry	3	1	51	34*	25.5
M. Gandy	3	0	47	28	15.7
M. Hoy	2	0	29	29	14.5

BOWLER	OVERS	MAIDENS	RUNS	WICKETS	AVERAGE
J. Pindolia	9.2	2	27	5	5.4
V. Nambiar	17	3	53	7	7.6
I. Shah	16	3	73	6	12.2

NOTABLE BATTING PERFORMANCES

PLAYER	OPPOSITION	SCORE
I. Shah	St. John's Northwood	145*

NOTABLE BOWLING PERFORMANCES

PLAYER	OPPOSITION	FIGURES
J. Pindolia	St. John's Northwood	2-12

Did you know? . . . In an effort to slow the scoring of the legendary Australian batsman Don Bradman on the 1932/3 tour of Australia, the England captain Douglas Jardine instructed his quick bowlers to bowl directly at the batsman's body. In defending himself, the batsman was liable to be caught by the close-fielders.

The tactic became known as 'Bodyline' and the series remains one of cricket's darkest hours. Soon afterwards the laws of cricket were changed to limit the number of fielders behind square on the leg-side.

THE ORATORY

Goring Heath, Reading, RG8 7SF

Tel: 0118 9844511 Fax: 0118 9844806

Email: office@oratoryprep.co.uk

Headmaster: D.L. Sexon   Master i/c Cricket: J.G.M. Derrett

2005 SEASON

Played: 10   Won: 3   Lost: 2   Drawn: 5

Captain: C. Whittaker Vice-captain: B. Mitchell

Team selected from: C. Whittaker*, B. Mitchell*, T. Huysinga*, A. Anker, F. Payne, T. Willson, A. Fitzpayne, A. Johnston, D. Brownlee, B. Henderson, B. Jennings, D. Wilson, C. Keogh, T. Richards, J. Thurston.

Scorer: R. Nolan

SUMMARY

Of the XI that were to meet Caldicott in the first fixture of the season, only three had represented the school at this level in the previous year. A ten wicket win against Caldicott, including a school record 178 for the first wicket, was an excellent start. The following fixtures against St. Andrews, Cheam, Crosfields and The Beacon were all drawn. Despite setting good totals, a lack of early season penetration meant we were unable to break other teams resolve.

A loss against St. John's Beaumont highlighted some bowling and fielding inadequacies. A win in the last over against Moulsford was followed by a frustrating draw against Claires Court. In a wet encounter at St. Hugh's we won a low-scoring match before being defeated in our last fixture against The Dragon. Chasing 199-6 our batsmen never looked settled against an impressive spin attack on a very dry wicket as we were bowled out for 90 – our lowest total of the summer.

A good season with a lot of runs but we found maintaining pressure difficult at times. Coupled with missed chances in the field, this excellent side did not close out some of the matches it should have done.

AVERAGES

BATSMAN	INNINGS	NOT OUT	RUNS	H. SCORE	AVERAGE
C. Whittaker	9	3	274	66	45.7
T. Huysinga	10	2	316	80	39.5
B. Mitchell	10	1	316	121*	35.1
A. Johnston	5	2	59	30*	19.7
T. Willson	9	1	126	46	15.8
B. Henderson	5	0	68	27	13.6

BOWLER	OVERS	MAIDENS	RUNS	WICKETS	AVERAGE
B. Mitchell	73	10	272	20	13.6
C. Whittaker	76	10	304	14	21.7
A. Fitzpayne	60.4	10	220	8	27.5
T. Willson	14	0	114	3	38.0
D. Brownlee	31.1	2	167	3	55.7
F. Payne	25	5	115	2	57.5

WICKET-KEEPER	PLAYED	CAUGHT	STUMPED
B. Henderson	9	9	1

NOTABLE BATTING PERFORMANCES

PLAYER	OPPOSITION	SCORE
B. Mitchell	Caldicott	121*
T. Huysinga	Crosfields	80
T. Huysinga	The Beacon	68
C. Whittaker	The Beacon	66
C. Whittaker	St. John's Beaumont	60*
T. Huysinga	Claires Court	50*
B. Mitchell	Crosfields	50

NOTABLE BOWLING PERFORMANCES

PLAYER	OPPOSITION	FIGURES
B. Mitchell	St. Hugh's	4-16
C. Whittaker	Cheam	4-18
B. Mitchell	St. Andrew's	4-19
B. Mitchell	Crosfields	4-33
B. Mitchell	Moulsford	3-18
C. Whittaker	St. Hugh's	3-23
C. Whittaker	Caldicott	3-28

ORLEY FARM

South Hill Avenue, Harrow on the Hill, Middlesex HA1 3NU

Tel: 020 8869 7604 Fax: 020 8869 7601

Email: office@orleyfarm.harrow.sch.uk

Headmaster: I. Elliott Master i/c Cricket: J. Labuschagne

2005 SEASON

Played: 5   Won: 4   Drawn: 1

Captain: A. Poole   Vice-captain: A. Nanavati

Team selected from: R. Majithia*, S. Cato*, A. Poole*, G. Bhambra*, A. Nanavati*, C. Clarke, L. Allen, S. Patel, A. Kutner, D. Wijesinghe, S. Radia.

SUMMARY

Only the first match, drawn against St. John's, was a close encounter. The other games were won by the comfortable margins of 193 runs against Arnold House, 137 runs against Aldwickbury, 8 wickets against The Hall and 6 wickets against St. Martin's. The top five batsmen saw most of the action. The openers, Sam Cato and Rishi Majithia, consistently put together solid partnerships which allowed Alex Poole licence to play his array of powerful strokes. His 55 fours and 17 sixes in 5 innings rather tell the story. Arjun Nanavati always batted sensibly when required and Gurkipal Bhambra contributed a belligerent 41 versus Aldwickbury.

Sam Cato opened the bowling with accurate out-swing, which was particularly effective against St. Martin's. Arnold House's top five were undone by the length and line of Saavan Radia and Shaneil Patel and the tail was mopped up by Dilan Wijesinghe. Alex Kutner showed promise with his tight in-swing. The bowling was backed up by some excellent fielding with memorable catches taken by Poole, Majithia and the keeper, Louis Allen, who was consistently tidy behind the stumps.

AVERAGES

BATSMAN	INNINGS	NOT OUT	RUNS	H. SCORE	AVERAGE
A. Poole	5	3	387	157*	193.5
R. Majithia	5	1	124	44	31.0
A. Nanavati	5	3	47	26	23.5
G. Bhambra	4	0	70	41	17.5
S. Cato	5	0	74	23	14.8

BOWLER	OVERS	MAIDENS	RUNS	WICKETS	AVERAGE
S. Radia	13	2	48	6	8.0
D. Wijesinghe	16	3	42	5	8.4
S. Cato	20.2	5	63	7	9.0
A. Poole	16	1	68	6	11.3
A. Kutner	18	5	48	4	12.0
S. Patel	17	2	79	4	19.8

WICKET-KEEPER	PLAYED	CAUGHT	STUMPED
L. Allen	5	6	0

NOTABLE BATTING PERFORMANCES

PLAYER	OPPOSITION	SCORE
A. Poole	Arnold House	157*
A. Poole	Aldwickbury	136*
R. Majithia	St. Martin's	44
A. Poole	The Hall	43*
G. Bhambra	Aldwickbury	41
R. Majithia	Arnold House	33
A. Poole	St. John's	34

NOTABLE BOWLING PERFORMANCES

PLAYER	OPPOSITION	FIGURES
S. Cato	St. Martin's	5-5
S. Radia	Arnold House	3-9
D. Wijesinghe	Arnold House	3-9

ORWELL PARK

Nacton, Ipswich, Suffolk IP10 0ER

Tel: 01473 659225 Fax: 01473 659822

Email: headmaster@orwellpark.co.uk

Headmaster: A. Auster   Master i/c Cricket: A. Auster

2005 SEASON

Played: 14   Won: 6   Lost: 4   Drawn: 4

Captain: F. Eccles-Williams   Vice-captain: G. Paton

Team selected from: F. Eccles-Williams*, G. Baylis, G. Berry, J. Bowden, O. Bunting*, G. Carton, H. Gravell*, G. Paton*, E. Prior, F. Rose, T. Rose*, C. Speakman.

Scorer: H. Northcroft-Brown

SUMMARY

With nine regular players of the 1st XI from the fifth form, there is great anticipation about the 2006 season, building on the success of 2005, which included the retention of the U12 County Championship.

Good wins were secured in a most positive fashion, in four matches by margins of over 100 runs (Barnardiston Hall, Haileybury, St. Joseph's College, Woodbridge)! The school were on the receiving end against a very strong Felsted side in a match where extras were top scorer for Orwell with 26! The most thrilling victory was achieved against Royal Hospital with Freddie Rose and Charlie Speakman taking Orwell from 96-9 to the winning total of 129 - a great last-wicket partnership. A new record 5th wicket partnership was also set this season by Gregor Paton and Hugo Gravell who put on 117 against Woodbridge school.

Thanks are due to coaches Adam Seymour and Brian Hunt, to the matronal department for the 'whitest of whites' match kit, to the catering team for their excellent match teas, and to the ground staff for producing such fabulous wickets.

AVERAGES

BATSMAN	INNINGS	NOT OUT	RUNS	H. SCORE	AVERAGE
G. Paton	13	1	314	63	26.2
T. Rose	11	1	261	56*	26.1
H. Gravell	13	2	268	74*	24.4
O. Bunting	14	1	268	80*	20.6

BOWLER	OVERS	MAIDENS	RUNS	WICKETS	AVERAGE
T. Rose	72.3	9	262	27	9.7
F. Rose	58	9	184	15	12.3
F. Eccles-Williams	33.1	3	135	10	13.5
O. Bunting	64	8	244	17	14.4

WICKET-KEEPER	PLAYED	CAUGHT	STUMPED
H. Gravell	14	2	10

NOTABLE BATTING PERFORMANCES

PLAYER	OPPOSITION	SCORE
O. Bunting	Barnardiston Hall	80*
H. Gravell	Woodbridge	74*
G. Paton	Woodbridge	63
H. Gravell	Beeston Hall	72*
T. Rose	King's College Cambridge	54
T. Rose	Old Buckenham Hall	56*
O. Bunting	Ipswich	60

NOTABLE BOWLING PERFORMANCES

PLAYER	OPPOSITION	FIGURES
O. Bunting	Barnardiston Hall	5.2-1-14-4
O. Bunting	Barnardiston Hall	8-1-15-4
O. Bunting	Old Buckenham Hall	4.4-0-27-4
G. Paton	Woodbridge	4.4-1-6-4
T. Rose	Royal Hospital	12-4-24-5
T. Rose	St. Joseph's	4-0-14-4

PAPPLEWICK

Ascot, Berkshire SL5 7LH

Tel: 01344 621488 Fax: 01344 874639

Email: hm@papplewick.org.uk

Headmaster: T. Bunbury   Master i/c Cricket: Martin Barker

2005 SEASON

Played: 18   Won: 6   Lost: 10   Drawn: 2

Captain: W. Talkington   Vice-captain: Y. Sert

Team selected from: W. Talkington*, S. Foster, Y. Sert*,
J. Brooks*, W. Harrison, C. Miller-Stirling, B. Thompson*,
J. Regan, J. Lowsley-Williams, T. Osibodu, L. Sullivan.

SUMMARY

A memorable season in many respects, not least because 2005 was a touring year with the venue being South Africa once again. The tour proved to be hard work on the field, although progress was made with the last two matches being won. The last match of the tour will live in the memory for years. On a perfect Cape Town day we played eight hours of cricket at the famous Constantia Uitsig ground and it all went to the last over of the day.

The team's performances did prove erratic throughout, with some excellent batting marred by some very undisciplined showings. The bowling lacked direction for much of the time although one thing you could be guaranteed were some high scoring matches!

The player who stood out was undoubtedly Yunus Sert who easily scored the most runs and was the second highest wicket-taker. He will be a force to be reckoned with in the side next year. All in all a very enjoyable season, with some very enthusiastic boys who evidently enjoyed their cricket.

AVERAGES

BATSMAN	INNINGS	NOT OUT	RUNS	H. SCORE	AVERAGE
Y. Sert	17	5	516	73*	43.0
J. Brooks	18	0	317	68	17.6
W. Talkington	18	1	275	59	16.2
B. Thompson	15	1	122	22	8.7
S. Foster	16	1	96	38	6.4
W. Harrison	14	0	83	32	5.9

BOWLER	OVERS	MAIDENS	RUNS	WICKETS	AVERAGE
W. Harrison	66	8	273	20	13.6
J. Lowsley-Williams	131.3	21	436	27	16.1
Y. Sert	172.4	27	553	26	21.3
B. Thompson	56.3	5	259	11	23.5
L. Sullivan	85	7	347	14	24.8
T. Osibodu	54	3	266	9	29.6

WICKET-KEEPER	PLAYED	CAUGHT	STUMPED
J. Brooks	18	7	6

NOTABLE BATTING PERFORMANCES

PLAYER	OPPOSITION	SCORE
Y. Sert	Summer Fields	51
Y. Sert	The Ridge (South Africa)	51
W. Talkington	Ludgrove	59
Y. Sert	Cranleigh	73*
J. Brooks	Lambrook Haileybury	68
J. Brooks	Josca's	50
Y. Sert	Josca's	54*

NOTABLE BOWLING PERFORMANCES

PLAYER	OPPOSITION	FIGURES
J. Lowsley-Williams	Blue Leopards (South Africa)	5-8

PINEWOOD

Bourton, Swindon, Wiltshire SN6 8HZ

Tel: 01793 782205 Fax: 01793 783476

Email: office@pinewoodschool.co.uk

Headmaster: P. Hoyland Master i/c Cricket: Dan Gazard

2005 SEASON

Played: 8 Won: 3 Lost: 2 Drawn: 3

Captain: O. Davies Vice-captain: M. Manners

Team selected from: O. Davies*, M. Manners*, E. Mason*,
R. Bethwaite, G. Cooper, E. Folland, H. Zinupoulos,
L. Dempster, D. Ivory, F. Upton, M. MacLeod, W. Grant,
H. Blanshard, A. Jeffcut.

SUMMARY

This year's squad had the potential to produce one of our finest teams for years. Our batting promised to be exciting and destructive and on its day did not disappoint. In the early season, Owen Davies proved himself to be the pick of the batsmen with 96 against Prior Park and 57* against Josca's. As the season progressed, Matty Manners produced glimpses of his undoubted talent and Eddy Mason finished off the season with two fifties. Rory Bethwaite has technique, a straight bat and a good mental approach.

Our bowling attack did not quite have the penetration or pace to bowl good sides out on a regular basis. Openers Eddy Mason and Harry Zinupoulos bowled with control and were able to frustrate. Liam Dempster bowled his leg-spin with flight and guile while Rory Bethwaite bowled a flatter more containing leg-spin. Dan Ivory worked hard to give the side an off-spinning option. Felix Upton and George Cooper gave us even more variety. The side worked hard on its fielding and the ground fielding in particular. With just two defeats this was an enjoyable season.

NOTABLE BATTING PERFORMANCES

PLAYER	OPPOSITION	SCORE
O. Davies	Prior Park	96
O. Davies	Josca's	57*
E. Mason	Wycliffe College	53
E. Mason	St. Hugh's	63*

RED LEATHER

by Andrew Fraser

As the young faces wait for 'Sir' at the nets, practising this season's bowling action, the cricket master appears from deep within the school with a plastic bag in one hand and a cricket bat in the other. The bat is interesting but it is the bag on which their eyes alight. For all the attention they give it, a casual observer might wonder what sugary delights are contained therein. As they delve inside the bag of practice balls it's every boy for himself. They are not after last year's crop of match balls, which are worn and rust-red, nor do they want those recovered by the headmaster's dog from the winter undergrowth.

A new cricket ball has an enduring magic. It has the appeal of the forbidden fruit of fairy-tales, a juicy four and three-quarter ounce braeburn or fairground toffee-apple. On match days the umpire produces the ball from the his coat like a greengrocer proffering his finest fruit in that strange crinkly see-through paper. At once the schoolboy opening bowler knows he is privileged to be allowed the first 'bite'.

As a youngster one soon grows out of the 'Granny Smith' tennis ball. It is soft to the touch but appears dulled and bitter to the eye. It comes off the bat with a 'pop', rather that the throaty 'thwack' of leather. The age-old 'six and out' of garden cricket is always overshadowed by the threat of 'break a pane - end of game'. Many a week's pocket-money has been lost as ten-year-olds learn the glazing trade before their time.

The cricket ball remains a prized possession at prep school, a reward for those first achievements on the field, a buddy to help pass the time between the nominative and the ablative, a good luck charm in the inkwell of the exam desk. The tell-tale red stain on the trousers explains that low mark in the French vocabulary test. Like another of its kind, the conker, it soon fades or is lost, but that initial attraction crosses the generations as surely as night follows day.

Trendy as reverse-swing may be at the present time, there's unlikely to be a schoolboy in the country who would take a well-used ball over a brand-new nugget of 'red leather'.

PORT REGIS

Motcombe Park, Shaftesbury, Dorset SP7 9QA
Tel: 01747 852566 Fax: 01747 854684
Email: office@portregis.com
Headmaster: P.A.E. Dix   Master i/c Cricket: Phil Lawrence

2005 SEASON

Played: 13   Won: 6   Lost: 2   Drawn: 5

Captain: T. Cooke   Vice-captain: R. Loveridge

Team selected from: T. Cooke*, R. Loveridge*, E. Bonnell*,
A. Jeffreys, J. Nieboer, J. Carlile, C. van der Meulen,
J. Francis, E. Routh, W. Felton, H. Wilson, G. Wayman.

Scorer: L. Renouf

SUMMARY

There was an excellent team spirit and atmosphere prevalent in this side. These qualities, together with excellent fielding, swung the balance in several tight victories.

Theo Cooke took the most wickets and scored the most runs. His bowling spells against Sandroyd (5-7), Victoria College and Pridwin were especially devastating. He also top-scored on four occasions. A good all-rounder, Edward Bonnell, contributed significantly, his 59 against Clayesmore and 4-13 against Sherborne being particularly memorable. Alex Jeffreys and Joshua Nieboer both top-scored twice. Rufus Loveridge took more catches than anyone - several of them simply stunning - and made a committed all-round contribution. James Carlile contributed too with bat (most notably against Pridwin) and ball, while Henry Wilson recorded bowling figures of 3-1 against Farleigh and Edward Routh often impressed behind the stumps.

Of those returning next season, James Francis, Christopher van der Meulen, George Wayman and William Felton all showed real promise for the future.

AVERAGES

BATSMAN	INNINGS	NOT OUT	RUNS	H. SCORE	AVERAGE
T. Cooke	10	3	207	50*	29.6
E. Bonnell	12	4	196	59	24.5
A. Jeffreys	8	1	103	47	14.7
J. Nieboer	11	2	108	28	12.0
J. Carlile	7	3	36	19*	9.0

BOWLER	OVERS	MAIDENS	RUNS	WICKETS	AVERAGE
C. van der Meulen	28	2	83	12	6.9
T. Cooke	71.3	18	185	20	9.3
H. Wilson	27.2	3	83	6	13.8
E. Bonnell	55.5	10	172	12	14.3
R. Loveridge	28	5	94	6	15.7
J. Francis	60.4	14	198	12	16.5

WICKET-KEEPER	PLAYED	CAUGHT	STUMPED
E. Routh	10	1	0
G. Wayman	2	1	0

NOTABLE BATTING PERFORMANCES

PLAYER	OPPOSITION	SCORE
E. Bonnell	Clayesmore	59
T. Cooke	Clayesmore	50*
A. Jeffreys	St. Michael's	47
T. Cooke	Chafyn Grove	42
T. Cooke	Millfield	37
A. Jeffreys	Sherborne	33
J. Nieboer	Pridwin (South Africa)	28

NOTABLE BOWLING PERFORMANCES

PLAYER	OPPOSITION	FIGURES
T. Cooke	Sandroyd	5-7
J. Francis	Farleigh	5-15
C. van der Meulen	St. Michael's	4-6
E. Bonnell	Sherborne	4-13
H. Wilson	Farleigh	3-1
T. Cooke	Victoria College	3-2
T. Cooke	All Hallows	3-12

St. ANDREW'S

Meads, Eastbourne, East Sussex BN20 7RP

Tel: 01323 733203 Fax: 01323 646860

Email: office@androvian.biblio.net

Headmaster: J.R.G. Griffith   Master i/c Cricket: Mike Harrison

2005 SEASON

Played: 6   Won: 3   Drawn: 3

Captain: J. Hyder

Team selected from: B. Saunders, S. Ford, P. Wooldridge, J. Curd, J. Hyder, D. Arwas, D. Smart, C. Borsoi, T. Brace, H. Porpora, C. Wickramarachchi, M. Robinson, N. Chreleda, O. Hyne.

SUMMARY

Accurate bowling, excellent fielding and a very good team ethic were the reasons for the successes achieved during this season. A comfortable win against Brambletye was set up through the efforts of new leg-spinner J. Curd (3-3). A victory against St. Bede's followed, with tight bowling from Wooldridge and Curd and a quick-fire 54* off 23 balls from the captain Hyder. A tense draw against Vinehall ensued, having set a modest total of 134 for 8. Vinehall soon reached 122-2 and all seemed lost. Three fine overs from Smart and Borsoi redressed the balance and Vinehall ended on 133-6.

Against Ashdown House we had another tense draw. Having been set a target of 145 the top order was removed without fuss and at 40-5 from 7 overs the game was too difficult to win against a strong Ashdown attack, which bowled a creditable 39 overs. A dogged partnership between Borsoi and Porpora held firm for 21 overs.

Brighton College made a deserved total of 165-3 with some excellent stroke play. In reply, Wooldridge was the mainstay, his 48* ensuring the draw. A convincing win against Windlesham House at the end of the season left us undefeated.

AVERAGES

BATSMAN	INNINGS	NOT OUT	RUNS	H. SCORE	AVERAGE
J. Hyder	3	0	113	54*	37.7
P. Wooldridge	3	0	96	48*	32.0
J. Curd	1	0	30	17*	30.0
B. Saunders	5	0	61	20	12.2

BOWLER	OVERS	MAIDENS	RUNS	WICKETS	AVERAGE
D. Smart	16	0	59	5	11.8
J. Curd	20	3	85	7	12.1
D. Arwas	21	4	54	4	13.5
P. Wooldridge	24	7	66	3	22.0

NOTABLE BATTING PERFORMANCES

PLAYER	OPPOSITION	SCORE
J. Hyder	St. Bede's	54*
P. Wooldridge	Brighton College	48*

NOTABLE BOWLING PERFORMANCES

PLAYER	OPPOSITION	FIGURES
C. Curd	Brambletye	3-3
P. Wooldridge	St. Bede's	2-8
C. Borsoi	Vinehall	3-24

Did you know? . . . The highest and lowest England Test totals were made in Ashes Tests. At the Oval in 1938 England finished on 903-7 declared, while in Sydney, in 1886-87, they were dismissed for 45.

S. ANSELM'S

Bakewell, Derbyshire DE45 1DP

Tel: 01629 812511 Fax: 01629 814742

Email: headmaster@anselms.co.uk

Headmaster: R. J. Foster Master i/c Cricket: C. J. Acheson-Gray

2005 SEASON

Played: 11   Won: 7   Lost: 2   Drawn: 2

Captain: W. Street

Team selected from: W. Street*, S. Spurrier*, M. White*,
R. Ho Chan*, J. Boyce*, J. Gregory, J. Brown, S. Leese,
C. Salloway, C. Dennis, W. Inglis, J. Wildgoose.

Scorer: T. Dunn

SUMMARY

Only twelve boys represented the 1st XI this term and only
William Street, the captain, had any first team experience. All
the boys contributed to the success of the side and they soon
developed into a tight-knit unit.

In a season where all our matches were timed cricket rather
than limited-overs, it was good to see that only two of the
eleven fixtures were drawn. In the two games that we lost, the
matches went to the final over of the day, with both sides in
with a chance of victory.

The senior players all made contributions, notably Sam
Spurrier (282 runs at 35.2) and William Street (27 wickets at
9.8). Ricky Ho Chan kept wicket tidily, James Boyce bowled
with a lot of pace and aggression and Max White was a reliable
opening batsman.

With four of the 1st XI (C. Salloway, W. Inglis, C. Dennis
and J. Wildgoose) returning we have the nucleus of a good side
in 2006.

AVERAGES

BATSMAN	INNINGS	NOT OUT	RUNS	H. SCORE	AVERAGE
S. Spurrier	10	2	282	60*	35.3
W. Street	10	4	191	74*	31.8
J. Gregory	8	1	133	58*	19.0
R. Ho Chan	11	1	186	50*	18.6
M. White	10	0	158	48	15.8

BOWLER	OVERS	MAIDENS	RUNS	WICKETS	AVERAGE
C. Dennis	38	6	108	15	7.2
W. Inglis	46	4	122	16	7.6
J. Boyce	35	8	116	15	7.7
W. Street	80	14	265	27	9.8

WICKET-KEEPER	PLAYED	CAUGHT	STUMPED
R. Ho Chan	11	7	1

NOTABLE BATTING PERFORMANCES

PLAYER	OPPOSITION	SCORE
W. Street	Pinewood	74*
S. Spurrier	Mount St. Mary's	60*
J. Gregory	Grace Dieu	58*
R. Ho Chan	Mount St. Mary's	50*
W. Street	Hill House	50*
S. Spurrier	Hill House	50*

NOTABLE BOWLING PERFORMANCES

PLAYER	OPPOSITION	FIGURES
W. Street	St. Crispin's	5-9
W. Inglis	Lichfield Cathedral	4-5
C. Dennis	Foremarke Hall	4-19
W. Street	Ranby House	4-34

St. AUBYN'S

76 High Street, Rottingdean, East Sussex BN2 7JN

Tel: 01273 302170 Fax: 01273 304004

Email: office@staubyns-school.org.uk

Headmaster: A.G. Gobat Master i/c Cricket: Shaun Greet

2005 SEASON

Played: 10   Won: 5   Lost: 1   Drawn: 4

Captain: A. Burrows Vice-captain: N. Carter

Team selected from: A. Burrows*, N. Carter*, J. Maennling*, A. Bishop, V. Clements, C. Line, F. Woodcock, J. Marshall, W. Wright, H. Parfitt, P. Chun, J. Saxby, B. Hickey.

Scorer: B. Calliafas

SUMMARY

After a poor start to the season and with eighteen boys from which to choose, it looked like it would be a long hard term. The fact that through sheer hard work and determination they turned things around and ended up with an impressive record, is testament to the character which existed within the group.

In the field, to a man, they were enthusiastic, alert and really supportive of each other. With both bat and ball somebody usually managed to turn in a useful performance, but much was owed to the 'lesser lights' whose support in every match was invaluable.

The names listed in the averages would not have achieved without the support of all the players in the team.

AVERAGES

BATSMAN	INNINGS	NOT OUT	RUNS	H. SCORE	AVERAGE
A. Burrows	9	3	356	102*	59.3
J. Maennling	8	2	220	85*	36.7
N. Carter	9	1	93	48	11.6

BOWLER	OVERS	MAIDENS	RUNS	WICKETS	AVERAGE
N. Carter	43	13	137	11	12.5
J. Maennling	56	7	232	17	13.6
A. Burrows	62	7	252	14	18.0
A. Bishop	33	5	169	8	21.1

WICKET-KEEPER	PLAYED	CAUGHT	STUMPED
C. Line	9	2	1

NOTABLE BATTING PERFORMANCES

PLAYER	OPPOSITION	SCORE
A. Burrows	Hurstpierpoint College	86*
N. Carter	Hurstpierpoint College	48
A. Burrows	Copthorne	79
J. Maennling	Mowden	51
A. Burrows	Cumnor House	102*
A. Bishop	St. Ronan's	40*
J. Maennling	St. Ronan's	43*

NOTABLE BOWLING PERFORMANCES

PLAYER	OPPOSITION	FIGURES
J. Maennling	Copthorne	4-5
F. Woodcock	Mowden	5-8
A. Bishop	St. Ronan's	4-35
A. Burrows	Great Ballard	3-11
N. Carter	Hurstpierpoint College	3-25
J. Maennling	Great Ballard	3-14

St. FAITH'S

Trumpington Road, Cambridge, CB2 2AG
Tel: 01223 352073 Fax: 01223 314757
Email: mcritchley@stfaiths.co.uk
Headmaster: S. Drew Master i/c Cricket: M. Critchley

2005 SEASON

Played: 10   Won: 3   Lost: 2   Drawn: 5

Captain: T. Andrews   Vice-captain: M. Horsford

Team selected from: T. Andrews*, C. Chambers, M. Counsell*,
A. Gale, J. Horsford, M. Horsford*, P. Miller,
S. Montague-Fuller, C. Newlove*, G. Otterman, J. Sandford*,
G. Skinner, M. York*.

SUMMARY

St. Faith's recorded excellent wins against King's Ely, Bedford
and Wellingborough. The latter provided the most complete
performance of the season. Chris Newlove and Patrick Miller
put on 160, by some distance the biggest partnership of the
year. A disciplined bowling and fielding performance saw the
boys home by 117 runs. A problem throughout much of the
season was a lack of consistency from the bowlers. The team
often failed to build pressure on opposition batsmen and bowled
too many 'four' balls. The side performed extremely well at the
Brandeston Hall Festival, narrowly losing to Norwich School in
the final.

Mark Horsford at last showed his class with the bat to back
up his outstanding wicket-keeping, whilst Andrew Gale took the
award for the bowler of the tournament with four wickets in
each game. The boys also reached the final of the Gresham's
Festival where they were defeated by a fine Clifton Durban XI.
Max York and James Sandford were the outstanding fielders
and their superb throwing caused several run-outs. Tom
Andrews led the side superbly, ably supported by Mark
Horsford.

AVERAGES

BATSMAN	INNINGS	NOT OUT	RUNS	H. SCORE	AVERAGE
J. Sandford	7	1	158	46*	26.3
P. Miller	8	2	126	56*	21.0
A. Gale	8	1	144	36	20.6
C. Newlove	10	1	184	96*	20.4
M. Counsell	7	0	140	40	20.0
M. Horsford	10	0	183	73	18.3

BOWLER	OVERS	MAIDENS	RUNS	WICKETS	AVERAGE
S. Montague-Fuller	30	2	102	8	12.7
J. Sandford	30	1	132	10	13.2
T. Andrews	44.5	4	177	11	16.1
M. Counsell	12	1	55	3	18.3
M. York	24	1	144	4	36.0
A. Gale	34	2	205	4	51.2

WICKET-KEEPER	PLAYED	CAUGHT	STUMPED
M. Horsford	10	7	0

NOTABLE BATTING PERFORMANCES

PLAYER	OPPOSITION	SCORE
C. Newlove	Wellingborough	96*
M. Horsford	Clifton (South Africa)	73
P. Miller	Wellingborough	56*
J. Sandford	King's Ely	46*
J. Sandford	St. John's	42
G. Skinner	Felsted	41
M. Counsell	Woodleigh	40

NOTABLE BOWLING PERFORMANCES

PLAYER	OPPOSITION	FIGURES
T. Andrews	King's Ely	4-2
T. Andrews	Wellingborough	3-15
J. Sandford	The Ridge (South Africa)	3-27
S. Montague-Fuller	Felsted	3-33
C. Chambers	King's Ely	2-1
M. Counsell	Wellingborough	2-8
S. Montague-Fuller	Wellingborough	2-19

St. HUGH'S

Carswell Manor, Faringdon, Oxon SN7 8PT

Tel: 01367 870700 Fax: 01367 870711

Email: headmaster@st-hughs.co.uk

Headmaster: D. Cannon   Master i/c Cricket: Greg Dasgupta

2005 SEASON

Played: 12   Won: 6   Lost: 6

Captain: J. West

Team selected from: J. West*, H. Sparks*, O. Lloyd*,
J. Benbow*, J. McRobert, W. Lloyd, J. Baldwin, T. Barton,
G. Sandbach, T. Ward, W. Harvey, R. Owen, H. Copson.

SUMMARY

Playing very positive cricket, our season consisted of many close, exciting games. There was talk of 'pay to view' as match after match went to the final over to decide the winner. No games were drawn and perhaps with slightly more resilient batting we could have saved a few games.

Our bowling and fielding were very good and we took ten wickets in seven of our twelve matches. A notable hat trick was taken by Josh Benbow against Beaudesert Park and crippling swing-bowling by Jack McRobert earned him 4-18 versus Ashfold. Jack, Will, George and Richard kept the art of spin alive, developing their consistency as the season progressed. With the bat our top order did most of the scoring, Tom and George scoring a total of 574 runs between them. Tom's 71* versus Moulsford was the top score of the season and as both return next year I hope they can better this.

All in all a great deal of credit must go to the players who really performed well as a team.

AVERAGES

BATSMAN	INNINGS	NOT OUT	RUNS	H. SCORE	AVERAGE
T. Barton	12	1	312	71*	28.4
J. Benbow	8	2	167	50	27.8
G. Sandbach	11	0	262	59	23.8
H. Sparks	8	1	101	51*	14.4
J. West	12	0	138	37	11.5

BOWLER	OVERS	MAIDENS	RUNS	WICKETS	AVERAGE
H. Sparks	33	8	90	7	12.9
T. Ward	40	4	153	10	15.3
J. Benbow	33	4	114	7	16.3
J. West	33	3	120	7	17.1

WICKET-KEEPER	PLAYED	CAUGHT	STUMPED
W. Harvey	11	5	1

NOTABLE BATTING PERFORMANCES

PLAYER	OPPOSITION	SCORE
T. Barton	Josca's	63
T. Barton	Moulsford	71*
G. Sandbach	Josca's	59
J. Benbow	The Dragon	50

NOTABLE BOWLING PERFORMANCES

PLAYER	OPPOSITION	FIGURES
J. McRobert	Ashfold	4-18

St. HUGH'S

Cromwell Avenue, Woodhall Spa, Lincolnshire LN10 6TQ
Tel: 01526 354964 Fax: 01526 351520
Email: office@sthughs.biblio.net
Headmaster: S. Greenish Master i/c Cricket: M. Brotherton

2005 SEASON

Played: 7   Won: 2   Lost: 1   Drawn: 4

Captain: D. Stevens

Team selected from: D. Stevens*, G. White, R. Clark, E. Bake,
R. Padley, J. Harris, J. Winwright, J. Clark, G. Chaggar,
J. Lang, E. Seabourne, M. Overton.

SUMMARY

This was an extraordinary and outstanding season for the team.
As ever, selection from a very small number of boys in Years 7
and 8 was difficult. However the team collectively played well
above expectations, losing just one game, and even that came
down to us reducing the opposition to nine wickets down, but
unable to take the tenth before the required runs were eeked out.

The batting statistics look poor, but we were not called upon
to bat a great deal. We bowled first in all but one match,
reducing most opposition to very few runs. We bowled superbly
all season but also collected an astonishing twelve run outs,
eight of which were direct hits.

Our fielding was quite superb all year. In total the team took
58 wickets in seven games at an average of eight runs per
wicket! There were many highlights: direct hits on the stump
from distance and Edward Bake's spell of 4-4-0-3 along with
those of Edward Seabourne (6.2-2-8-4) and Josh Lang (4-1-4-2
- all in different matches. A superb year culminating in winning
the Pocklington six-a-side.

AVERAGES

BATSMAN	INNINGS	NOT OUT	RUNS	H. SCORE	AVERAGE
D. Stevens	7	1	71	33	11.8
J. Harris	6	4	21	9*	10.5
E. Bake	4	1	29	23	9.7
R. Clark	4	1	29	18	9.7

BOWLER	OVERS	MAIDENS	RUNS	WICKETS	AVERAGE
E. Bake	11	7	5	5	1.0
E. Seabourne	43.2	7	126	13	9.7
J. Harris	32	2	116	12	9.7
J. Winwright	12	1	41	4	10.2
J. Lang	26	2	88	8	11.0
D. Stevens	34	5	92	4	23.0

WICKET-KEEPER	PLAYED	CAUGHT	STUMPED
R. Padley	6	2	4

NOTABLE BATTING PERFORMANCES

PLAYER	OPPOSITION	SCORE
D. Stevens	Hill House	33
G. White	Witham Hall	19
E. Bake	Hill House	23

NOTABLE BOWLING PERFORMANCES

PLAYER	OPPOSITION	FIGURES
E. Seabourne	Ranby House	6.2-2-8-4
J. Harris	Bramcote Lorne	4-2-4-4
E. Bake	Hill House	4-4-0-3
D. Stevens	Hill House	6-2-17-2
J. Lang	Boston GS	4-1-4-2

St. JOHN'S

Potter Street Hill, Northwood, Middlesex HA6 3QY
Tel: 020 8866 0067 Fax: 020 8868 8770
Email: office@st-johns.org.uk
Headmaster: C.R. Kelly   Master i/c Cricket: S. Murphy

2005 SEASON

Played: 12   Won: 5   Lost: 4   Drawn: 3

Captain: H. Franks   Vice-captains: J. Franks and G. MacKay

Team selected from: H. Franks*, J. Franks*, G. MacKay*,
G. Goulden*, B. Kakkad*, R. Samani*, B. Abrahams*,
J. Patel*, A. Mavani*, Y. Sheikh*, R. Davda, K. Singh.

Scorer: T. Arch

SUMMARY

This season saw our 1st XI defeated for the first time since July
2002! The team had a great deal of potential but performances
tended to be erratic. Jamie Patel could develop into a very able
left-handed batsman. His 63 against John Lyon was probably
the best individual innings of the season. Greg MacKay is a
very useful all-rounder - he got into the sixties on three
occasions and also claimed 16 wickets with his medium-paced
deliveries, including a hat trick against The Downs. Harry
Franks, the captain, played well throughout the season and his
captaincy improved from match to match.

The 2006 season should be very interesting as the 1st XI
will be a very young unit.

AVERAGES

BATSMAN	INNINGS	NOT OUT	RUNS	H. SCORE	AVERAGE
G. MacKay	10	0	223	61	22.3
H. Franks	11	1	168	50	16.8
B. Abrahams	9	3	100	31*	16.7
J. Patel	11	0	176	63	16.0
R. Samani	10	0	140	37	14.0

BOWLER	OVERS	MAIDENS	RUNS	WICKETS	AVERAGE
G. MacKay	60	17	209	16	13.1
Y. Sheikh	57	10	184	12	15.3
H. Franks	57	10	245	15	16.3
B. Kakkad	68	10	259	11	23.5

WICKET-KEEPER	PLAYED	CAUGHT	STUMPED
J. Franks	11	3	3

NOTABLE BATTING PERFORMANCES

PLAYER	OPPOSITION	SCORE
G. MacKay	John Lyon	60
J. Patel	John Lyon	63
G. MacKay	Northwood	61
G. MacKay	Merchant Taylors'	61
H. Franks	St. Martin's	50

NOTABLE BOWLING PERFORMANCES

PLAYER	OPPOSITION	FIGURES
Y. Sheikh	Davenies	4-2-23-4
H. Franks	Davenies	9-2-23-4
B. Kakkad	Merchant Taylors'	8-1-23-4

St. JOHN'S BEAUMONT

Priest Hill, Old Windsor, Berkshire SL4 2JN

Tel: 01784 432428   Fax: 01784 494048
Email: secretary@stjohnsbeaumont.co.uk

Headmaster: D. Gogarty   Master i/c Cricket: G. Baguley

2005 SEASON

Played: 13   Won: 11   Drawn: 2

Captain: J. Richardson   Vice-captain: Z. Ansari

Team selected from: J. Richardson*, Z. Ansari*, S. Beasant*,
M. Ehmer*, A. Pindar*, C. McInerney*, L. Marjason,
A. Rudzitis, W. Eaves, J. Mitchell, M. Wilson, B. Bickford*.

Scorer: N. Hartman

SUMMARY

The 1st XI, having put in many hours of preparation, had a first-class season, undefeated after playing a total of thirteen matches. Throughout the season the the boys played positive cricket and thanks to their practice, commitment and skills were rewarded with some fine wins.

They were ably led by wicket-keeper, Jonathan Richardson, assisted by vice-captain, Zafar Ansari. They in turn were supported by numerous outstanding cricketers, ensuring some exciting matches. Two boys, Zafar Ansari and Maximillian Ehmer, scored centuries on two occasions. Zafar was also leading wicket-taker with thirty-eight wickets, backed up by Sebastian Beasant and Benjamin Bickford. The team fielded well and this is illustrated by the fact that run outs were the fourth highest wicket-taker.

All matches were played in a good spirit, with a particularly memorable victory over a South African touring side. On a scorching hot day, with conditions clearly favouring the visitors the 1st XI played imaginative cricket and bowled the opposition out for 91, having set a target of 156.

AVERAGES

BATSMAN	INNINGS	NOT OUT	RUNS	H. SCORE	AVERAGE
Z. Ansari	12	5	545	129*	77.9
M. Ehmer	13	4	618	117	68.7
B. Bickford	7	3	104	68	26.0
A. Pindar	9	4	78	30	15.6
S. Beasant	7	2	66	24	13.2
J. Richardson	10	1	110	34	12.2

BOWLER	OVERS	MAIDENS	RUNS	WICKETS	AVERAGE
Z. Ansari	97	32	196	38	5.2
C. McInerney	31	5	87	10	8.7
S. Beasant	62	11	200	19	10.5
B. Bickford	59	10	181	17	10.6
A. Pindar	51	9	145	8	18.1
L. Marjason	17	1	57	3	19.0

NOTABLE BATTING PERFORMANCES

PLAYER	OPPOSITION	SCORE
Z. Ansari	Oratory	129*
M. Ehmer	Oratory	117
M. Ehmer	St. John's	100*
Z. Ansari	Hall Grove	100*
Z. Ansari	The Dragon	83
Z. Ansari	Papplewick	80
Z. Ansari	WHPS	72

NOTABLE BOWLING PERFORMANCES

PLAYER	OPPOSITION	FIGURES
Z. Ansari	WHPS	6-3
Z. Ansari	Yateley Manor	5-6
Z. Ansari	The Beacon	5-27
Z. Ansari	The Dragon	5-40
Z. Ansari	Dulwich College	4-22
Z. Ansari	Aldro	3-3
Z. Ansari	Shrewsbury House	3-8

St. MARTIN'S

40 Moor Park Road, Northwood, Middlesex HA6 2DJ

Tel: 01923 825740 Fax: 01923 835452

Email: office@stmartins.org.uk

Headmaster: D. Tidmarsh   Master i/c Cricket: R. Moore

2005 SEASON

Played: 10   Won: 4   Lost: 4   Drawn: 2

Captain: S. Shah   Vice-captain: R. Kotecha

Team selected from: S. Merali*, B. Rajkumar*, H. Ripper, S. Shah*, R. Kotecha*, S. Taank, B. Makwana, H. Sheikh, E. Edwards, N. Patel, R. Mukadam, S. Klein, P. Shak.
Scorer: M. Marris

SUMMARY

The 1st XI contained a core of players from last year who were joined by some from last year's 2nd XI. The season started well with three wins over John Lyon, Aldenham and York House but of the remaining fixtures the side only managed one further victory. Aldwickbury were too strong for us, as were Orley Farm, despite a fine half-century from skipper Sajan Shan. A draw then followed against Lochinver House and a narrow defeat by 2 runs in the JET competition against Durstan House. We drew with St. John's before a fine victory over Westbrook Hay, who were dismissed for just over 70 runs with Rajiv Kotecha taking a hat trick.

The final game of the season saw a poor performance against Northwood Prep where batsmen tried to play extravagant strokes rather than building an innings. The future shows signs of promise with Year 7 boys in the 2nd XI and the Colts showing talent.

NOTABLE BATTING PERFORMANCES

PLAYER	OPPOSITION	SCORE
S. Shah	Orley Farm	54
S. Shah	Durstan House	38
B. Rajkumar	Lochinver House	45
S. Merali	York House	40

NOTABLE BOWLING PERFORMANCES

PLAYER	OPPOSITION	FIGURES
N. Patel	Aldenham	4-8
R. Kotecha	Westbrook Hay	5-4
S. Shah	St. John's	3-11

152

The Ashes *(Reproduced by kind permission of The MCC Museum)*
For details regarding guided tours of The MCC Museum contact 020 7616 8596

***Did you know?* . . .** At the end of their successful 1882-83 tour of Australia, the Hon Ivo Bligh's England team were presented with an urn by a group of Melbourne ladies. It was long thought that the contents were the ashes of a bail from the deciding Test of the series, but their true origin remains a mystery.

St. MARY'S

Abbey Park, Melrose, Roxburghshire TD6 9LN

Tel: 01896 822517 Fax: 01896 823550

Email: enquiries@stmarys.newnet.co.uk

Headmaster: J.A. Brett   Master i/c Cricket: I.P. Purvis

2005 SEASON

Played: 6   Won: 2   Lost: 3   Drawn: 1

Captain: E. Hardie

Team selected from: E. Hardie*, G. Wilson, R. Gogan,
T. Lonsdale, W. Sanderson, H. Goodson, D. Crawford,
A. Yellowlees, B. Waugh, P. Vint, A. Adams, J. McGowan,
S. Smith-Maxwell, J. Galbraith, F. Gogan.

SUMMARY

The 2005 season was comparatively short for St. Mary's. A handful of cancelled fixtures saw only six competitive matches for us during the summer term with varying degrees of success.

The season was full of potential and with such a small squad of players they were able to enjoy plentiful one-to-one coaching and with many being under eleven, I hold high hopes for the seasons to come.

Highlights weren't always in the winning but more in watching the young players grow in confidence, with both bat and ball. They all showed tremendous courage in facing up to some incredibly swift bowling attacks, notably Sunningdale, and special mentions have to go to Hugh Goodson and Peter Vint for defending their wickets so well on many occasions. Angus Adams had a catch dropped on a hat trick ball against Cargilfield and Barney Waugh's incredibly consistent length and line against Sunningdale was memorable.

Special mention must also go to Elliott Hardie for all his efforts and for ultimately picking up the school's batting, bowling and fielding prizes. Final thanks to John Brett and Reece Wearing for their support throughout.

NOTABLE BATTING PERFORMANCES

PLAYER	OPPOSITION	SCORE
E. Hardie	Fathers	50*
P. Vint	Inter School	74
W. Sanderson	Former Pupils	42
E. Hardie	Inter School	54

NOTABLE BOWLING PERFORMANCES

PLAYER	OPPOSITION	FIGURES
E. Hardie	Fathers	5-36
B. Waugh	Sunningdale	2-38
A. Adams	Cargilfield	3-15

Did you know? . . . Prior to England's Ashes victory in 2005, Australia had won the last eight series. Before Michael Vaughan, the last England captain to win the Ashes was Mike Gatting who led his side to a 2-1 series victory in Australia in 1986/7.

St. OLAVE'S

Clifton, York, YO30 6AS

Tel: 01904 527391 Fax: 01904 640975

Email: enquiries@st-olaves.york.sch.uk

Headmaster: A. Falconer   Master i/c Cricket: John Slingsby

2005 SEASON

Played: 12   Won: 6   Lost: 6

Captain: W. Peet   Vice-captain: H. Booth

Team selected from: W. Peet, S. Ash, H. Carr, J. Crossley,
A. Dickinson, B. Sykes, H. Booth, C. Code, D. McDermottroe,
C. McTurk, T. Peel, J. Tankard, J. Fletcher, H. Holmes,
W. Stephen, D. Green, W. Smith.

Scorer: G. Ng

SUMMARY

Looking at the scores throughout the season it is clear to see why this side did not win more than half its matches. They simply could not score enough runs. The team were happier batting first and setting a total. Too often the total was not large enough to give our varied attack a chance. The exception was Harry Booth, who is a very fine batsman, scoring freely on both sides of the wicket.

Bowling was varied and often put the opposition on the back foot. Tom Bilton bowled well and was supported by Alex Dickinson. The change bowling of Will Peet, Harry Booth and Josh Tankard was successful, especially the spin of Booth and Tankard.

The fielding, especially ground fielding, was good. Special mention to David McDermottroe, behind the stumps, and the speed of Chris McTurk in the covers.

NOTABLE BATTING PERFORMANCES

PLAYER	OPPOSITION	SCORE
H. Booth	St. Martin's	89
H. Booth	Silcoates	73
W. Peet	Barnard Castle	51

The Joint Educational Trust

JET was established as a charity in 1971 with Sir Douglas Bader as its first Chairman. JET is the only educational charity devoted to supporting the primary and middle school age groups who have boarding need. Supported entirely by voluntary donations, they help children who are unable to fulfil their potential because of family circumstances. JET places these children in schools best able to provide the necessary security and educational facilities and is responsible for funding these places.

The JET School Cricket Knockout Competition

The Joint Educational Trust School Cricket Competition was introduced in 1986 and since 1994 the finals have been hosted by St. Edward's Oxford. This year's semi-finalists, Millfield, Malsis, Durston House and Dulwich, made it through from the thirty-seven teams that entered the 25 over competition. After a good final the eventual winners were Millfield Preparatory School.

St. RICHARD'S

Bredenbury Court, Bromyard, Herefordshire HR7 4TD

Tel: 01885 483491 Fax: 01885 488982

Email: st.dix@virgin.net

Headmaster: R.E.H. Coghlan   Master i/c Cricket: Greg Harwood

2005 SEASON

Played: 14   Won: 5   Lost: 5   Drawn: 4

Captain: J. James   Vice-captain: W. Arbuthnott

Team selected from: J. James, W. Arbuthnott, J. Sherwood, H. Hames, P. O'Driscoll, D. Shough, A. Chester-Master, T. Whittal-Williams-Cotterell, J. Morgan, C. Phillips, S. Barrett, L. Page.

Scorer: A. MacLeod

SUMMARY

Our first match was against Moor Park. We bowled first and took an early wicket, but loosened our grip as they built up a good second wicket partnership. Despite their late wickets, they posted a score of 107. We batted slowly and uncertainly to force a draw.

In our next match against Brecon, we were all out for 82, which they reached with plenty of overs to spare. Then we played Hillstone who we dismissed for 141. Despite only losing four wickets, we ended ten runs short.

Our next match was against The Downs who we bowled out quickly for 54, and we then quickly reached their total. Then we played The Elms who made 86. In reply we closed on 68-9.

In our next matches we beat Abberley Hall 2nd XI and Moffats. At the height of the season we played S. Anselm's who hit a quick 141 and we could only muster a slow 91. In our final two fixtures we lost to Hereford and Moor Park.

AVERAGES

BATSMAN	INNINGS	NOT OUT	RUNS	H. SCORE	AVERAGE
J. James	9	4	235	65*	47.0
D. Shough	6	2	93	45	23.3
H. Hames	11	3	158	65*	19.8
S. Barrett	14	1	210	55	16.2

BOWLER	OVERS	MAIDENS	RUNS	WICKETS	AVERAGE
W. Arbuthnott	64	-	209	23	9.1
P. O'Driscoll	83	-	185	20	9.2
J. Sherwood	35	-	145	10	14.5
T. W-W-Cotterell	30	-	143	6	23.8
J. James	81	-	218	9	24.2

WICKET-KEEPER	PLAYED	CAUGHT	STUMPED
H. Hames	11	3	0

NOTABLE BATTING PERFORMANCES

PLAYER	OPPOSITION	SCORE
J. James	Hillstone	65*
H. Hames	Hereford	65*
J. James	Fathers	57*
S. Barrett	Moffats	55
J. James	Abberley Hall	44*

NOTABLE BOWLING PERFORMANCES

PLAYER	OPPOSITION	FIGURES
W. Arbuthnott	Down's	6-12
J. Sherwood	Hillstone	3-21
J. James	Hillstone	3-14
P. O'Driscoll	Moor Park	4-19

St. RONAN'S

Water Lane, Gun Green, Hawkhurst, Kent TN18 5DJ

Tel: 01580 752271 Fax: 01580 754882

Email: info@saintronans.co.uk

Headmaster: W.E.H. Trelawny-Vernon Master i/c Cricket: Ian Light

2005 SEASON

Played: 9   Won: 5   Lost: 3   Drawn: 1

Captain: E. Berger   Vice-captain: M. March

Team selected from: E. Berger*, M. March*, R. Blundell*, M. Thomas*, J. Gooderson, S. Hasan, O. Richards, J. Stow, T. Berger, C. Carter, J. Fisher, H. MacIntyre.

Scorer: W. Langer

SUMMARY

This has been an encouraging season after a slow start with two losses in 25 over matches. Most pleasing this season has been the batting which has enabled us to post some impressive scores, notably the 185-2 in just 24 overs against Claremont and the 165-1 in 22 overs against Mowden, but there were other solid performances as well.

In the bowling we had good strength in the seam department but could have done with a top quality spinner on occasions. The fielding was, generally, very good with some outstanding catches from Bertie Berger, Matt Thomas and Oscar Richards in particular.

AVERAGES

BATSMAN	INNINGS	NOT OUT	RUNS	H. SCORE	AVERAGE
E. Berger	8	1	212	100*	30.3
C. Carter	8	2	171	65*	28.5
M. Thomas	8	1	76	37*	10.9
O. Richards	6	1	53	36	10.6
M. March	6	1	38	11	7.6
T. Berger	5	0	27	14	5.4

BOWLER	OVERS	MAIDENS	RUNS	WICKETS	AVERAGE
H. MacIntyre	14	6	26	7	3.7
M. Thomas	13.3	2	34	8	4.2
J. Gooderson	14.1	4	41	8	5.1
E. Berger	50	13	123	19	6.5
O. Richards	22	1	75	7	10.7
C. Carter	35	10	67	4	16.7

WICKET-KEEPER	PLAYED	CAUGHT	STUMPED
T. Berger	9	3	2

NOTABLE BATTING PERFORMANCES

PLAYER	OPPOSITION	SCORE
E. Berger	Claremont	100*
E. Berger	St. Aubyn's	50
C. Carter	St. Aubyn's	50*
C. Carter	Mowden	65*
M. Thomas	Mowden	37*
O. Richards	St. Aubyn's	36

NOTABLE BOWLING PERFORMANCES

PLAYER	OPPOSITION	FIGURES
E. Berger	St. Aubyn's	4-2-4-5
E. Berger	Bethany	8-4-10-5
H. MacIntyre	St. Bede's	4-2-2-4
J. Gooderson	Mowden	4-0-13-4
M. Thomas	Milner Court	4-0-11-3

SANDROYD

Rushmore Park, Tollard Royal, Salisbury, Witshire SP5 5QD
Tel: 01725 516264 Fax: 01725 516441
Email: office@sandroyd.com
Headmaster: M.J. Harris Master i/c Cricket: Paul Fowler

2005 SEASON

Played: 10   Won: 6   Lost: 2   Drawn: 2

Captain: T. Kerridge   Vice-captain: C. Goodwin

Team selected from: T. Kerridge*, C. Goodwin*, R. Busher,
J. Kelway-Bamber*, H. Cheal*, W. Cave*, B. Thompson*,
C. Leach, M. MacKean, J. de Meo, F. Braithwaite-Exley.

Scorer: M. Watanabe

SUMMARY

This was a good team effort with a number of players chipping
in with runs and wickets. The team were a positive bunch
looking for the win on every occasion. Two matches were even
draws, both our defeats were comprehensive and six matches
were wins. The highlights were Robbie Busher's 96 against
Monkton Combe when he so deserved his elusive first ton.

Ben Thompson produced two match-winning bowling
performances against West Hill Park and Old Malthouse. The
most amazing performance was William Cave's 5-0 in ten balls
to turn a certain draw into an unlikely victory against Monkton
Combe.

Year 7 pupil Henry Cheal had a most encouraging season
with a forceful knock of 78 against the Old Malthouse. A good
season was always on the cards with six of last year's XI
returning. Only two boys will remain to form the basis of next
year's side.

AVERAGES

BATSMAN	INNINGS	NOT OUT	RUNS	H. SCORE	AVERAGE
R. Busher	9	2	239	96	34.1
T. Kerridge	10	2	179	53	22.4
J. Kelway-Bamber	7	2	108	41*	21.6
H. Cheal	9	2	144	78	20.6
C. Goodwin	8	2	85	30	14.2
W. Cave	8	1	101	26	14.4

BOWLER	OVERS	MAIDENS	RUNS	WICKETS	AVERAGE
C. Goodwin	42	6	120	14	8.6
W. Cave	35	6	104	11	9.5
R. Busher	58	13	147	15	9.8
B. Thompson	46.3	5	180	15	12.0
T. Kerridge	47.3	4	157	9	17.4

WICKET-KEEPER	PLAYED	CAUGHT	STUMPED
J. Kellway-Bamber	10	4	4

NOTABLE BATTING PERFORMANCES

PLAYER	OPPOSITION	SCORE
R. Busher	Sherborne	56*
H. Cheal	Old Malthouse	78
J. Kelway-Bamber	Old Malthouse	41*
R. Busher	Monkton Combe	96
T. Kerridge	Monkton Combe	53

NOTABLE BOWLING PERFORMANCES

PLAYER	OPPOSITION	FIGURES
B. Thompson	West Hill Park	6-15
B. Thompson	Old Malthouse	5-19
W. Cave	Monkton Combe	5-0
T. Kerridge	Westbourne House	4-34
R. Busher	Westbourne House	4-16

SOLEFIELD

Solefields Road, Sevenoaks, Kent TN13 1PH
Tel: 01732 452142 Fax: 01732 740388
Email: solefield.school@btinternet.com
Headmaster: P. Evans   Master i/c Cricket: R. Boyce

2005 SEASON

Played: 5   Won: 1   Lost: 1   Drawn: 3

Captain: T. Watts   Vice-captain: E. Woodhouse-Darry

Team selected from: R. Aitken, S. Cuterres*, T. Watts*,
E. Woodhouse-Darry*, F. Forward, G. Cuterres,
M. Harmon-Tatton*, S. Holland, W. Ellison-Smith*, J. Norton,
C. Thomas, J. Partridge.

SUMMARY

The Solefield season is, of necessity, a short one with a maximum of seven matches. This year was even shorter due to rain causing our first and last matches to be cancelled. This was a shame as with almost all of last year's XI back it promised much.

Due to the weather, our opening match was our first foray onto grass, the boys doing well to achieve the better of a draw.

We then lost a 15 over thrash by five runs. In our two strongest fixtures we suffered on an artificial wicket and a batting paradise, ending up with draws after chasing very high totals. Finally, we achieved a good win in what proved to be the last fixture. Overall there were no outstanding stars in the side but everyone pulled together to produce a strong unit.

AVERAGES

BATSMAN	INNINGS	NOT OUT	RUNS	H. SCORE	AVERAGE
E. Woodhouse-Darry	4	3	49	14*	49.0
S. Cuterres	4	1	77	37*	25.7

BOWLER	OVERS	MAIDENS	RUNS	WICKETS	AVERAGE
J. Norton	18	2	97	5	19.4
M. Harmon-Tatton	19	3	88	4	22.0
T. Watts	18	1	109	4	27.2

NOTABLE BATTING PERFORMANCES

PLAYER	OPPOSITION	SCORE
S. Cuterres	New Beacon	37*

NOTABLE BOWLING PERFORMANCES

PLAYER	OPPOSITION	FIGURES
T. Watts	Sevenoaks	2-8

Did you know? . . . Jim Laker's 19-90 for England against Australia at Manchester in 1956 are the best Test match bowling figures by any player. Tony Lock took the other wicket.

SOMERSET COLLEGE

P.O. Box 3512, Somerset West, 7129 South Africa

Tel: +2721 842 0050 Fax: +2721 842 0052

Email: cod@somcol.co.za

Headmaster: A. Wyborn   Master i/c Cricket: Richard Codrington

2005 SEASON

Played: 9   Won: 6   Lost: 3

Captain: C. Nel   Vice-captain: M. Versfeld

Team selected from: C. Nel, C. Koopman, K. Louw,
M. Versfeld, P. Fatzer, D. Arthur, N. Murrel, A. Becker,
B. Stephens, R. Klopper, N. Meinert,
L. Breytenbach, C. Johnstone.

Scorer: T. Agates

SUMMARY

A very busy 2005 season with some outstanding results including notable and historic victories over Somerset House, Beaumont and De Hoop. Highlights of the season included being runners-up in both the Wynberg Cricket Skills Tournament and in the day/night tournament. The team was well captained by Conrad Nel with tremendous performances at the crease from Martin Versfeld. This has been our best season in the short history of the school. We look forward 2006!

This season saw the second Somerset West Cricket Club U13 day/night competition. Six schools took part in the 30 over event held at Radloff Park. It is a beautiful setting and as dusk settles the braais are lit and the atmosphere increases with every ball bowled.

One semi-final was interrupted by thunder, lightning and rain and Messrs Duckworth and Lewis were nearly called, but happily the weather improved. The final was a tense affair between Somerset College and Dr Joubert Primary. Some outstanding cricket was played and a close game was enjoyed by the army of supporters. The last ball was not bowled until about 11.30pm with Dr Joubert Primary winning by 20 runs.

Playing under lights is a wonderful opportunity for the boys and they love the experience – any other takers out there?

AVERAGES

BATSMAN	INNINGS	NOT OUT	RUNS	H. SCORE	AVERAGE
M. Versfeld	8	2	274	89	45.7
C. Nel	5	2	115	54	38.3
A. Becker	3	1	31	17	15.5
D. Arthur	7	2	67	26	13.4
P. Fatzer	6	0	73	31	12.2
R. Klopper	2	0	16	15	8.0

BOWLER	OVERS	MAIDENS	RUNS	WICKETS	AVERAGE
N. Meinert	43	6	125	11	11.4
C. Nel	32	2	143	11	13.0
B. Stephens	14	2	94	7	13.4
P. Fatzer	27	3	138	10	13.8
M. Versfeld	40	5	162	10	16.2
D. Arthur	28	3	160	5	32.0

WICKET-KEEPER	PLAYED	CAUGHT	STUMPED
R. Klopper	-	-	-

NOTABLE BATTING PERFORMANCES

PLAYER	OPPOSITION	SCORE
M. Versfeld	Somerset West	89
C. Nel	Somerset House	43
M. Versfeld	Cornwall U13	42
M. Versfeld	Somerset House	43
C. Nel	De Hoop	54

NOTABLE BOWLING PERFORMANCES

PLAYER	OPPOSITION	FIGURES
N. Meinert	Beaumont	6-16
N. Meinert	Strand	4-13
C. Nel	Somerset West	4-16
N. Meinert	Somerset West	3-14
M. Versfeld	Strand	3-7
B. Stephens	Sir Lowry's Pass	3-17

SUMMER FIELDS

Mayfield Road, Oxford, OX2 7EN

Tel: 01865 454433 Fax: 01865 459200

Email: schoolsec@summerfields.org.uk

Headmaster: R.F. Badham-Thornhill

Master i/c Cricket: R.B. Lagden and M. Smith

2005 SEASON

Played: 14   Won: 9   Lost: 1   Drawn: 4

Captain: E. Gross   Vice-captain: H. Freyne

Team selected from: E. Gross*, H. Freyne*, T. Nelson*,
T. Faber*, W. Meakin*, H. Faber*, O. Jones*, N. Gill*,
J. Hallam*, G. Collard*, A. Nelson*, F. Leech.

Scorer: T. McAlpine

SUMMARY

As these results suggest, this was a most exciting and successful season for the XI - indeed it was the best season we have had for many a year. The first seven games were all won with victories against Beaudesert, Papplewick, Horris Hill, Elstree, Cheltenham, Moulsford and Abingdon. The most exciting of these saw us beat Papplewick with three balls to spare, thanks to a great stumping by Ollie Jones, standing up to Hector Freyne. Ironically, two of the drawn games were the two most exciting. Cothill held on for a draw and Caldicott were denied victory off the last ball, thanks to a catch on the long-off boundary by Henry Faber.

The team spirit was excellent and the side were very well led by Edmund Gross, who also starred with the bat and ball. He has been an outstanding prep school captain and player. He was ably assisted by Hector Freyne, whose left-arm over seam bowling was pretty useful, and by other senior players Tom Nelson, Tommy Faber, Hugo Meakin, Henry Faber and Nick Gill. Ollie Jones was an outstanding wicket-keeper and with George Collard, James Hallam and Archie Nelson, will form the foundations for 2006.

AVERAGES

BATSMAN	INNINGS	NOT OUT	RUNS	H. SCORE	AVERAGE
E. Gross	13	0	445	83	34.2
H. Freyne	13	3	227	39*	22.7
G. Collard	10	3	157	32	22.4
W. Meakin	10	3	150	42	21.4
T. Nelson	13	1	155	38*	12.9
T. Faber	13	1	139	38	11.6

BOWLER	OVERS	MAIDENS	RUNS	WICKETS	AVERAGE
E. Gross	95.2	18	236	31	7.6
H. Freyne	88.2	15	238	20	11.9
H. Faber	30	1	127	9	14.1
J. Hallam	46	8	131	7	18.7
N. Gill	57	8	192	10	19.2
T. Faber	41	2	189	9	21.0

WICKET-KEEPER	PLAYED	CAUGHT	STUMPED
O. Jones	11	4	10
T. Nelson	3	1	1

NOTABLE BATTING PERFORMANCES

PLAYER	OPPOSITION	SCORE
E. Gross	Abingdon	83
E. Gross	Horris Hill	81
E. Gross	Elstree	64
E. Gross	Moulsford	51
W. Meakin	Winchester House	42
H. Freyne	Moulsford	39*
T. Nelson	Cheltenham College	38*

NOTABLE BOWLING PERFORMANCES

PLAYER	OPPOSITION	FIGURES
H. Freyne	Papplewick	4-8
E. Gross	Abingdon	4-10
E. Gross	Winchester House	4-18
H. Freyne	Moulsford	4-14
E. Gross	Caldicott	4-42
H. Faber	Abingdon	3-14
E. Gross	Moulsford	3-9

SUNNINGDALE

Sunningdale, Berkshire SL5 9PY

Tel: 01344 620159 Fax: 01344 873304

Email: headmaster@sunningdaleschool.co.uk

Headmasters: A.J.N. & T.M.E. Dawson

Master i/c Cricket: T.M.E. Dawson

2005 SEASON

Played: 10   Won: 3   Lost: 2   Drawn: 5

Captain: J. Galbraith   Vice-captain: T. Witherow

Team selected from: J. Galbraith*, T. Witherow*,
W. Richardson*, G. Wheatley*, T. Turner,
Hon G. Bowes Lyon, H. Raikes, A. Phillpotts, S. Plunket,
R. Dhaliwal, R. Seevaratnam.

SUMMARY

We relied heavily on our two old colours, Galbraith and
Witherow, who made over half the runs and took almost two
thirds of the wickets. On top of this, Galbraith captained the
side with authority and set a splendid example in the field. We
had enough bowling. Wheatley and Bowes Lyon were both
quick, Witherow bowled left-arm spin and Galbraith and Turner
medium-pace. Our strike-rate, however, was simply not good
enough, in part because we dropped too many catches. The
opening pair were not supported by the middle order and
Richardson, who was capable of hitting the ball very hard, had a
disappointing season.

We did well to hold our own against Ludgrove, Cothill and
Horris Hill and had a most enjoyable and highly successful first
tour of Scotland.

AVERAGES

BATSMAN	INNINGS	NOT OUT	RUNS	H. SCORE	AVERAGE
J. Galbraith	10	4	200	44*	33.3
T. Witherow	10	0	182	64	18.2
G. Wheatley	4	1	39	16*	13.0
W. Richardson	10	1	99	30	11.0
A. Phillpotts	7	2	45	17*	9.0

BOWLER	OVERS	MAIDENS	RUNS	WICKETS	AVERAGE
T. Witherow	57	4	249	24	10.4
J. Galbraith	64.2	5	231	19	12.2
G. Wheatley	62	11	188	11	17.1
T. Turner	35.2	3	145	7	20.7
G. Bowes Lyon	49	9	168	7	24.0

WICKET-KEEPER	PLAYED	CAUGHT	STUMPED
W. Richardson	10	2	3

NOTABLE BATTING PERFORMANCES

PLAYER	OPPOSITION	SCORE
T. Witherow	Cothill	64
J. Galbraith	Bishopsgate	44*
J. Galbraith	Ludgrove	39*

NOTABLE BOWLING PERFORMANCES

PLAYER	OPPOSITION	FIGURES
T. Witherow	Bishopsgate	6-23
T. Witherow	Belhaven Hill	5-4
T. Witherow	St. Mary's	4-7
J. Galbraith	St. Mary's	4-14
J. Galbraith	Hall Grove	4-20

TERRINGTON HALL

Terrington, York, YO60 6PR

Tel: 01653 648227 Fax: 01653 648458

Email: headmaster@terringtonhall.com

Headmaster: J. Glen   Master i/c Cricket: T. Chapman

2005 SEASON

Played: 8   Won: 3   Lost: 3   Drawn: 2

Captain: W. Prest

Team selected from: W. Prest*, T. Brown, D. Glen,
J. Cordingley, J. Searle, L. Williams, T. Francis, H. Dixon,
H. Barnard, J. Prest, N. Fenwick, A. Green, A. Heald, P. Cronin.

Scorer: M. Rahtz

SUMMARY

This was a fairly modest season, both in terms of games played and victories recorded. The clear highlight was victory at Aysgarth (at last!).

The side was ably led by captain, William Prest, who was also the leading run-scorer and wicket-taker. No batsman scored a half-century but the captain reached the forties on two occasions. L. Williams scored a creditable 48 in the match against Aysgarth and D. Glen 42 against Bow.

Two bowlers managed four wickets in a match. William Prest took 4-13 against Aysgarth and T. Brown 4-37 versus Ampleforth.

AVERAGES

BATSMAN	INNINGS	NOT OUT	RUNS	H. SCORE	AVERAGE
W. Prest	6	1	145	44	29.0
H. Dixon	3	2	23	14	23.0
D. Glen	6	0	113	42	18.8
L. Williams	4	0	63	48	15.8
J. Prest	2	0	31	25	15.5
T. Brown	5	0	70	34	14.0

BOWLER	OVERS	MAIDENS	RUNS	WICKETS	AVERAGE
W. Prest	44	14	104	16	6.5
H. Barnard	17	3	56	6	9.3
T. Brown	25	3	116	9	12.9
D. Glen	23	1	122	9	13.6
N. Fenwick	22	5	83	5	16.6
J. Cordingley	33	3	107	5	21.4

NOTABLE BATTING PERFORMANCES

PLAYER	OPPOSITION	SCORE
W. Prest	Bramcote	44
W. Prest	Durham Choristers	42
L. Williams	Aysgarth	48
D. Glen	Bow	42

NOTABLE BOWLING PERFORMANCES

PLAYER	OPPOSITION	FIGURES
W. Prest	Aysgarth	7-2-13-4
T. Brown	Ampleforth College	8-1-37-4

TOCKINGTON MANOR

Tockington, Bristol, BS32 4NY

Tel: 01454 613229 Fax: 01454 613676
Email: admin@tockington.bristol.sch.uk

Headmaster: R.G. Tovey Master i/c Cricket: G. Witchard

2005 SEASON

Played: 6   Won: 1   Lost: 4   Drawn: 1

Captain: J. Durrans-Paul

Team selected from: J. Durrans-Paul, C. Blake, S. Taylor,
H. Williams, C. Brown, R. Tucker, A. Martinez, J. Checa,
J. Smith, J. King, J. Baio, H. Rose, J. Parsonage,
E. Ford, J. Hawker.
Scorer: J. Hawker

SUMMARY

In my first season as 1st XI coach I really didn't know what to expect. During the first couple of training sessions there seemed to be some budding cricketers and others who would possibly struggle through the season.

James King, James Durrans-Paul and Alvaro Martinez, the find of the season, gave plenty of encouragement with the bat. Against St. Ursula's in the last match, Alvaro showed what a great eye he has for hitting the ball. The bowlers, like Charlie Blake, Sebastian Taylor and James Parsonage deserve recognition for their spells of bowling. The captain, James Durrans-Paul, deserves credit for the way he led the side. It is not easy to captain a side that is full of school friends and try to please all of them, but he seemed to do this very well. Thank you also to Josh Hawker for his scoring.

The Wycliffe six-a-side tournament was an experience; we tried our best but came up against some very strong sides. As in most games we were consistently unable to score enough runs, or restrict the batting side when bowling first, to create any sort of pressure on the opposition.

AVERAGES

BATSMAN	INNINGS	NOT OUT	RUNS	H. SCORE	AVERAGE
A. Martinez	4	1	43	31*	14.3
J. King	5	1	53	21	13.3
J. Durrans-Paul	6	0	59	26	9.8
C. Blake	6	1	36	25*	7.2
J. Smith	5	1	26	17*	6.5

BOWLER	OVERS	MAIDENS	RUNS	WICKETS	AVERAGE
S. Taylor	18	0	78	6	13.0
J. Smith	10	0	64	3	21.3
J. Parsonage	21.3	2	86	3	28.7
C. Blake	21.5	1	106	3	35.3

NOTABLE BATTING PERFORMANCES

PLAYER	OPPOSITION	SCORE
A. Martinez	St. Ursula's	31*
J. Durrans-Paul	Beaudesert Park U12	26
J. King	Beaudesert Park U12	21
C. Blake	St. John's Cardiff	25*
J. King	St. Ursula's	20*

NOTABLE BOWLING PERFORMANCES

PLAYER	OPPOSITION	FIGURES
J. Smith	St. Ursula's	3-8
J. Checa	St. Ursula's	2-3
J. Parsonage	Beaudesert Park U12	2-7
S. Taylor	St. John's Cardiff	2-14
J. King	St. John's Cardiff	2-11
S. Taylor	St. John's Chepstow	2-9
C. Blake	The Elms	2-27

WELLINGBOROUGH

Irthlingborough Road, Wellingborough, Northamptonshire NN8 2BX

Tel: 01933 222698 Fax: 01933 233474

Email: prep-head@wellingboroughschool.org

Headmaster: R. Mitchell Master i/c Cricket: R.W.H. Smith

2005 SEASON

Played: 11   Won: 6   Lost: 2   Drawn: 3

Captain: J. Moxham   Vice-captain: J. Johnson

Team selected from: J. Moxham*, J. Johnson*, S. McGuire*, N. Joshi*, W. Knibbs*, A. Waring*, J. Collins, M. Dallimore, J. Cliffe, W. Bigley, R. Patel, D. Fitzhugh.

SUMMARY

The 1st XI have had another fine season. They have approached their practices and matches with great dedication. They won five of their matches but lost heavily to St. Faith's and Norwich School. The side's success was built around the batting of Jack Johnson, Joe Moxham and Sam McGuire. All three of them scored runs regularly and they all have the ability to do well in the future.

The highlights were Jack's 125 against Bedford and Joe and Sam's 186 run stand against Maidwell. All the bowlers bowled consistently well with Joe Moxham, Alex Waring and William Knibbs taking regular wickets. Neil Joshi showed the worth of a good spinner. On the whole the fielding was very good with Josh Cliffe, William Bigley and Sam McGuire setting a high standard. The captain, Joe Moxham, had an exceptional season. He has a good understanding of the game and he led the side with great maturity.

AVERAGES

BATSMAN	INNINGS	NOT OUT	RUNS	H. SCORE	AVERAGE
J. Johnson	6	4	292	125	146.0
J. Moxham	9	2	276	82	39.4
S. McGuire	7	1	180	71*	30.0
W. Bigley	7	0	97	33	13.9

BOWLER	OVERS	MAIDENS	RUNS	WICKETS	AVERAGE
J. Moxham	64	6	197	23	8.6
N. Joshi	56	12	161	17	9.5
A. Waring	72	13	216	16	13.5
W. Knibbs	61	8	194	11	17.6

WICKET-KEEPER	PLAYED	CAUGHT	STUMPED
J. Johnson	8	5	3

NOTABLE BATTING PERFORMANCES

PLAYER	OPPOSITION	SCORE
J. Johnson	Bedford	125
J. Moxham	Maidwell Hall	82
J. Johnson	Stoneygate	79*
S. McGuire	Maidwell Hall	71*

NOTABLE BOWLING PERFORMANCES

PLAYER	OPPOSITION	FIGURES
A. Waring	Maidwell Hall	5-11
N. Joshi	Bilton Grange	6-16
J. Moxham	Kimbolton	5-24
N. Joshi	Beeston Hall	4-10
W. Knibbs	Beeston Hall	4-10
J. Moxham	Maidwell Hall	4-23

WELLOW HOUSE

Wellow, Newark, Nottinghamshire NG22 0EA

Tel: 01623 861054 Fax: 01623 836665

Email: wellowhouse@btinternet.com

Headmaster: P. Cook   Master i/c Cricket: Nick Forbes

2005 SEASON

Played: 9   Won: 6   Lost: 2   Drawn: 1

Captain: J. Cooper   Vice-captain: L. Fisher

Team selected from: J. Cooper*, L. Fisher*, M. Dixon, H. Perks, D. Stanford, O. Blow, E. Hill, J. Taylor, A. Jennings, A. Barson, H. Ainscough, M. Buckland, J. Cullingham, M. Napier, H. Tacey.

Scorer: P. Sunderland

SUMMARY

Joe Cooper captained the side enthusiastically, with some innovative field-placing. Luke Fisher bowled excellent line and length and Max Dixon was stylish behind the stumps.

With three young players leaving early, who will fill the gap? Joe carried the side through on the strength of his batting, strong all round the wicket, especially punishing of anything short. The lower order were unable to back him up.

AVERAGES

BATSMAN	INNINGS	NOT OUT	RUNS	H. SCORE	AVERAGE
J. Cooper	9	2	366	72*	52.3
H. Perks	5	2	45	24	15.0
J. Taylor	5	0	71	34	14.2
L. Fisher	9	1	109	36	13.6

BOWLER	OVERS	MAIDENS	RUNS	WICKETS	AVERAGE
L. Fisher	65	9	173	31	5.6
J. Cooper	64	9	156	20	7.8

WICKET-KEEPER	PLAYED	CAUGHT	STUMPED
M. Dixon	9	4	2

NOTABLE BATTING PERFORMANCES

PLAYER	OPPOSITION	SCORE
J. Cooper	Hill House	72*
J. Cooper	Grace Dieu	64
J. Cooper	Grosvenor	55
J. Cooper	Lincoln Minster	54

NOTABLE BOWLING PERFORMANCES

PLAYER	OPPOSITION	FIGURES
L. Fisher	Bramcote	6-9
L. Fisher	Grosvenor	6-25
J. Taylor	Mount St. Mary's	3-4

WESTBOURNE HOUSE

Shopwyke, Chichester, West Sussex PO20 2BH

Tel: 01243 782739 Fax: 01243 770759

Email: whouseoffice@rmplc.co.uk

Headmaster: B.G. Law   Master i/c Cricket: Kevin Smith

2005 SEASON

Played: 12   Won: 10   Lost: 1   Drawn: 1

Captain: G. Holman   Vice-captain: W. Langmead

Team selected from: G. Holman, W. Langmead, J. Michael, S. Grant, J. Lighton, A. Pusinelli, G. Cussins, H. Lloyd, J. Breton, J. Pretorius, H. Lighton, H. Briggs.

SUMMARY

Another very successful season for the XI. The introduction of limited overs in home matches made for many more exciting games and the opportunity for the boys to play positive cricket at all times. There were many outstanding team and individual performances throughout the campaign and everyone played their part to develop an excellent spirit.

The batting had plenty of depth, although all the leading stroke-makers were vulnerable early in their innings and consistency was a problem. The bowling was varied but sometimes lacked penetration and accuracy. To finish the season we were able to repay some of the outstanding hospitality we received in South Africa by hosting Crawford Prep School from Durban.

AVERAGES

BATSMAN	INNINGS	NOT OUT	RUNS	H. SCORE	AVERAGE
S. Grant	9	5	175	52*	43.8
J. Michael	10	3	235	55*	33.6
W. Langmead	11	2	250	101*	27.8
A. Pusinelli	7	2	130	40	26.0
G. Holman	11	2	170	37	18.9

BOWLER	OVERS	MAIDENS	RUNS	WICKETS	AVERAGE
J. Pretorius	54	6	190	21	9.0
H. Lighton	63	10	152	16	9.5
J. Michael	27	4	90	9	10.0
A. Pusinelli	55	12	141	13	10.8
J. Lighton	41	8	141	11	12.8
G. Cussins	35	3	112	4	28.0

WICKET-KEEPER	PLAYED	CAUGHT	STUMPED
G. Holman	11	12	2

NOTABLE BATTING PERFORMANCES

PLAYER	OPPOSITION	SCORE
J. Michael	Aldro	55*
W. Langmead	Twyford	101*
S. Grant	Highfield	52*
J. Michael	Dorset House	44*

NOTABLE BOWLING PERFORMANCES

PLAYER	OPPOSITION	FIGURES
J. Pretorius	Seaford College	5-6
J. Lighton	Pilgrims	5-10
H. Lighton	Twyford	4-12

WINCHESTER HOUSE

44 The High Street, Brackley, Northamptonshire NN13 7AZ
Tel: 01280 702483 Fax: 01280 706400
Email: office@winchester-house.org
Headmaster: M.S. Seymour Master i/c Cricket: C.R. Wilson

2005 SEASON

Played: 10   Won: 2   Lost: 7   Drawn: 1

Captain: C. Drinkwater Vice-captain: E. Pointon

Team selected from: C. Drinkwater*, E. Pointon*, M. Johnson*,
O. Trotter*, W. Berner, P. Gregory, P. Adams, P. Morrissey,
A. Neasham, O. Strong, T. Huddart, T. Saunders, J. Crampton.

Scorer: J. Miles Ogden

SUMMARY

The XI had a good season, playing some aggressive cricket,
striving for wins regardless of any losses. The bowling proved
to be the strength, with four bowlers averaging under 20.
William Berner bowled accurately and fast in tandem with
Edward Pointon's leg-spin. The highlight of the bowling was
Edward's hat trick against Bedford.

The batting was less consistent but Miles Johnson batted
very well for long periods of time, culminating in two half-
centuries, one of which was part of a 123 run partnership with
Charlie Drinkwater.

In the field, Ollie Trotter led by example from behind the
stumps, making sure everything look tidy, while Paul Gregory
excelled in the outfield.

With six of the team returning next year, things look
promising for the future.

AVERAGES

BATSMAN	INNINGS	NOT OUT	RUNS	H. SCORE	AVERAGE
W. Berner	10	3	145	40*	20.7
M. Johnson	10	0	195	53	19.5
O. Trotter	10	2	150	35	18.8
C. Drinkwater	8	0	133	48	16.6
T. Saunders	2	0	28	25	14.0
P. Gregory	8	0	109	45	13.6

BOWLER	OVERS	MAIDENS	RUNS	WICKETS	AVERAGE
W. Berner	67	15	192	14	13.7
E. Pointon	66.3	11	283	20	14.2
T. Huddart	32.5	4	155	9	17.2
C. Drinkwater	36.1	7	139	7	19.9
M. Johnson	8	0	61	2	30.5
O. Trotter	40.2	6	188	5	37.6

WICKET-KEEPER	PLAYED	CAUGHT	STUMPED
O. Trotter	10	3	1
A. Neasham	10	3	2

NOTABLE BATTING PERFORMANCES

PLAYER	OPPOSITION	SCORE
M. Johnson	South Northants	51
M. Johnson	Northampton	53
C. Drinkwater	South Northants	48
C. Drinkwater	Moulsford	43
P. Gregory	Ashdown House	45
W. Berner	Caldicott	40*
M. Johnson	Caldicott	42

NOTABLE BOWLING PERFORMANCES

PLAYER	OPPOSITION	FIGURES
E. Pointon	Bedford	5-31
E. Pointon	Caldicott	5-49

WINTERFOLD HOUSE

Chaddesley Corbett, Worcestershire DY10 4PW

Tel: 01562 777234 Fax: 01562 777078

Email: hm@winterfoldhouse.co.uk

Headmaster: W. Ibbetson-Price Master i/c Cricket: G. Haynes

2005 SEASON

Played: 7   Won: 2   Lost: 3   Drawn: 2

Captain: M. Wyres

Team selected from: M. Wyres, B. Buckley, S. Cheshire, B. Hornsey, T. Russell-Brown, M. Gwillam, M. Shephard, T. Turner, N. Robbins, J. Bloomer, E. Cartwright, J. Walker, B. Robinson, C. Clarke, J. Rymer, D. Roache.

SUMMARY

The season tended to follow the same format, good bowling and fielding, but batting proving to be a problem. One of the draws and one of the defeats could so easily have been victories if just one batsman could have gone on to make a substantial contribution. On the other hand, a couple of the draws could have ended in defeat but for the dogged determination of the lower middle-order. There were some very good bowling performances. Ben Buckley and Michael Wyres in particular put us in good positions to win matches.

The final playing record was probably a fair analysis of the season. The pleasing point was the improvement and we were undefeated in our last four matches. Not many of our players play cricket outside school and so to compete in the matches as we did was a testament to the side's effort and enthusiasm.

AVERAGES

BATSMAN	INNINGS	NOT OUT	RUNS	H. SCORE	AVERAGE
J. Walker	5	0	63	24	12.6
B. Hornsey	7	1	66	20*	11.0
M. Wyres	6	1	49	17*	9.8
B. Buckley	5	0	47	22	9.4
S. Cheshire	6	2	32	17*	8.0
M. Gwillam	4	1	20	8*	6.7

BOWLER	OVERS	MAIDENS	RUNS	WICKETS	AVERAGE
M. Wyres	47.5	13	68	15	4.5
B. Buckley	31	9	67	11	6.1
J. Walker	14.2	2	52	2	26.0
T. Russell-Brown	39	3	140	5	28.0
J. Bloomer	15	0	59	2	29.5
M. Gwillam	12.2	2	31	1	31.0

WICKET-KEEPER	PLAYED	CAUGHT	STUMPED
B. Hornsey	7	1	0

NOTABLE BATTING PERFORMANCES

PLAYER	OPPOSITION	SCORE
B. Hornsey	St. Richard's	20*
J. Walker	Abberley Hall	24
B. Buckley	Moffats	22
J. Walker	Moffats	21
B. Hornsey	Hillstone	20

NOTABLE BOWLING PERFORMANCES

PLAYER	OPPOSITION	FIGURES
M. Wyres	St. Richard's	5-9
M. Wyres	The Elms	4-7
B. Buckley	Bredon	4-8

WOODCOTE HOUSE

Snows Ride, Windlesham, Surrey GU20 6PF

Tel: 01276 472115 Fax: 01276 472890

Email: info@woodcotehouseschool.co.uk

Headmaster: N.H.K. Paterson Master i/c Cricket: A.G. Monk

2005 SEASON

Played: 14 Won: 5 Lost: 2 Drawn: 7

Captain: J. Tomlinson Vice-captain: S. Aldridge

Team selected from: J. Tomlinson*, S. Aldridge*, M. Siredzuk*, J. Warman*, G. Chattey, M. Wallis, P. Cunliffe, A. Wauchope, F. Jenkins, H. Wright, T. MacFarlane, G. Lineker, J. Major.

Scorer: B. Trimble

SUMMARY

Four of the fourteen matches went to the last over with all four results possible. Four others were very one-sided. The other six matches were entertaining and positive encounters.

The highlight was chasing down the 142 set by Ashdown House, with Joe Warman and Matt Siredzuk sharing an undefeated seventh wicket stand of 53. The final visit from Sunningdale resulted in an eight wicket victory with Sam Aldridge scoring 52*. Sam also top-scored against St. Andrew's Pangbourne with 78 as he and skipper Joss Tomlinson (40) put on 134 for the first wicket.

Woodcote's three spinning 'Ws', Wauchope, Wright and Warman, took wickets with a variety of styles, with George Chattey, Sam Aldridge and Paddy Cunliffe providing the pace.

Two batting disasters, against Ludgrove and Hall Grove, were the only blemishes on a tremendous season which will be remembered fondly for the positive cricket displayed.

AVERAGES

BATSMAN	INNINGS	NOT OUT	RUNS	H. SCORE	AVERAGE
M. Siredzuk	11	4	217	60*	31.0
J. Warman	12	4	206	51*	25.8
S. Aldridge	13	1	296	78	24.7
G. Chattey	10	2	104	35	13.0
J. Tomlinson	11	2	92	40	10.2
M. Wallis	11	3	81	22*	10.1

BOWLER	OVERS	MAIDENS	RUNS	WICKETS	AVERAGE
H. Wright	41	8	146	15	9.7
J. Warman	43	8	130	12	10.8
G. Chattey	85	9	280	23	12.2
A. Wauchope	29	2	110	9	12.2
P. Cunliffe	15	2	68	5	13.6
S. Aldridge	46	4	196	12	16.3

WICKET-KEEPER	PLAYED	CAUGHT	STUMPED
M. Siredzuk	12	8	2
G. Lineker	2	1	2

NOTABLE BATTING PERFORMANCES

PLAYER	OPPOSITION	SCORE
S. Aldridge	St. Andrew's Pangbourne	78
J. Tomlinson	St. Andrew's Pangbourne	40
S. Aldridge	Dorset House	38
M. Siredzuk	St. George's Windsor	60*
P. Cunliffe	Dolphin	42
S. Aldridge	Sunningdale	52*
F. Jenkins	Parkside	37

NOTABLE BOWLING PERFORMANCES

PLAYER	OPPOSITION	FIGURES
H. Wright	Ludgrove	6-0-20-4
J. Warman	St. Andrew's Pangbourne	10-3-10-5
G. Chattey	Dorset House	8-1-10-4
H. Wright	Dorset House	8-6-13-4
G. Chattey	Dolphin	4-2-1-4
J. Warman	Sunningdale	6-3-4-4

WYCLIFFE COLLEGE

Ryeford Hall, Stonehouse, Gloucestershire GL10 2LD

Tel: 01453 852809 Fax: 01453 825604

Email: john.newns@wycliffe.co.uk

Headmaster: A. Palmer   Master i/c Cricket: J. Newns

2005 SEASON

Played: 11   Won: 6   Lost: 3   Drawn: 2

Captain: E. Price   Vice-captain: T. Wand

Team selected from: E. Price*, T. Wand*, W. Clapham*,
R. Woodmason, N. Morris, J. Kimber, A. Parker,
S. Barnett, R. Llewellyn, J. Chillingworth,
T. Edwards, J. Pearson.

SUMMARY

After a difficult few years the 2005 team restored some pride in school cricket. The batsmen scored runs and broke records. Our highest score of 216-2 was achieved against Tockington and we successfully chased targets in excess of 150 on three occasions. We had three century partnerships with Tom Wand featuring in all of them. His contribution of 334 runs has only been bettered once in the last twenty-seven years.

The bowling restrictions of eight overs means that it is now a batsman's game against small schools but Jack Kimber bowled brilliantly all season, conceding very few runs and having all sorts of batsmen in trouble. He was ably supported by Ed Price and Richard Woodmason.

The fielding improved considerably during the season and Seb Barnett, Tom Edwards and Will Clapham all saved runs in a good team effort. The highlights of the season were the victories against Cheltenham College where we chased 162 to win with Jack Kimber scoring 72 out of 105 in nine overs and the one wicket win against The City of London Freemen's School, again chasing a total of over 150 to win.

AVERAGES

BATSMAN	INNINGS	NOT OUT	RUNS	H. SCORE	AVERAGE
A. Parker	6	4	91	41*	45.5
E. Price	11	3	297	65	37.1
T. Wand	10	1	334	78*	37.1
J. Kimber	9	1	215	72	26.9
J. Pearson	7	3	98	66*	24.5

BOWLER	OVERS	MAIDENS	RUNS	WICKETS	AVERAGE
J. Kimber	78	29	133	20	6.6
R. Woodmason	76	8	254	19	13.4
E. Price	63	5	253	18	14.1
N. Morris	38	2	190	11	17.3

NOTABLE BATTING PERFORMANCES

PLAYER	OPPOSITION	SCORE
T. Wand	Hillstone	60*
E. Price	Hillstone	65*
J. Pearson	Tockington Manor	66*
T. Wand	Tockington Manor	78*
T. Wand	Cheltenham College	60
J. Kimber	Cheltenham College	72
T. Wand	City of London Freemen's	59

NOTABLE BOWLING PERFORMANCES

PLAYER	OPPOSITION	FIGURES
J. Kimber	Clifton College	4-5
J. Kimber	Pinewood	4-13
R. Woodmason	Pinewood	4-13
E. Price	Beaudesert Park	5-20
E. Price	St. John's	4-22
N. Morris	Tockington Manor	4-20

YARDLEY COURT

Somerhill, Tonbridge, Kent TN11 0NJ

Tel: 01732 352124 Fax: 01732 363381

Email: office@yardleycourt.kent.sch.uk

Headmaster: J. Coakley   Master i/c Cricket: A. Fritter

2005 SEASON

Played: 13   Won: 9   Lost: 2   Drawn: 2

Captain: J. Payne   Vice-captain: R. Harbig

Team selected from: J. Payne, R. Harbig, W. McDowell,
N. Spurling, S. Spencer, W. Maidman, M. Lindsay-Bayley,
N. Brauer, A. Pollard, J. Orchard, C. Farrant.

Scorer: A. Fritter

SUMMARY

A very good season for the 1st XI which included amongst the
nine victories winning the Hazelwood U13 'sixes' tournament.
There were also some fine wins against Vinehall, Sevenoaks
Prep, St. Michael's, Hawthorn and Solefield, climaxing with a
superb five wicket victory over a very strong Holmewood
House 1st XI.

Other highlights to mention include a superb 180* by Josh
Payne in a 20 over match versus Sevenoaks Prep. His
partnership for the fourth wicket with Nick Spurling was worth
an amazing 191 runs! Josh also scored a sublime 105* against
Solefields. He is certainly a name to watch out for in the future.
So, all in all, a very pleasing season with some superb cricket
being played at times. We look forward to season 2006.

AVERAGES

BATSMAN	INNINGS	NOT OUT	RUNS	H. SCORE	AVERAGE
J. Payne	10	2	445	180*	55.6
C. Farrant	6	3	123	69*	41.0
W. McDowell	12	2	310	85	31.0
N. Spurling	9	2	206	70	29.5
R. Harbig	11	2	188	50*	20.9

BOWLER	OVERS	MAIDENS	RUNS	WICKETS	AVERAGE
C. Farrant	32	4	112	9	12.4
N. Spurling	12	3	51	4	12.7
J. Payne	43	2	187	11	17.0
W. McDowell	41	7	164	9	18.2
R. Harbig	35.2	3	158	11	14.4

WICKET-KEEPER	PLAYED	CAUGHT	STUMPED
W. Maidman	13	4	1

NOTABLE BATTING PERFORMANCES

PLAYER	OPPOSITION	SCORE
J. Payne	Sevenoaks	180*
J. Payne	Solefield	105
W. McDowell	St. Michael's	85
J. Payne	Ashdown House	76
W. McDowell	Rose Hill	61
W. McDowell	Holmewood House	59*
N. Spurling	Hazelwood	70

NOTABLE BOWLING PERFORMANCES

PLAYER	OPPOSITION	FIGURES
M. Lindsay-Bayley	St. Michael's	3-11
J. Orchard	Hazelwood	3-1
R. Harbig	Bethany	3-13
W. McDowell	Bethany	3-9
J. Payne	Holmewood House	3-23

Fielding Positions
for a right-handed batsman

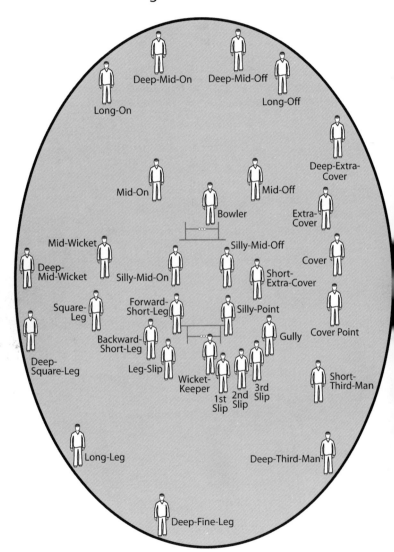